A LOVE SUPREME

A LOVE SUPREME

Real-Life Stories of Black Love

TaRessa & Calvin Stovall

FOREWORD BY RUBY DEE

WARNER BOOKS

A Time Warner Company

Warner Books, Inc., 1271 Avenue of the Americas, New York, NY 10020
Visit our Web site at www.twbookmark.com

 A Time Warner Company

Printed in the United States of America
First Printing: February 2000
10 9 8 7 6 5 4 3 2 1

Photo Credits:
Cover & p. 118, Dixie D. Vereen; p. 4, John Manning; p. 6, James Coley; p. 14, Robert Gary; p. 34 Raymond Williams; p. 54, D'Angelo Dixon; p. 59, Nick Arroyo, Atlantic Journal-Constitution; p. 68, Bud Smith; p. 71, Spelman College Archives; p. 123, Ivan Fritsch; p. 157, Susan J. Ross; p. 160, Debra A. Meeks; p. 167, Juan Garcia, Dallas Moring News; p. 185, William F. George; p. 202, Alex Morgan.

For a listing of permissions see page 217.

Library of Congress Cataloging-in-Publication Data

Stovall, TaRessa.
    A love supreme : real-life stories of Black love / TaRessa and
Calvin Stovall.
      p. cm.
   ISBN 0-446-52171-X
    1. Marriage—United States.   2. Afro-Americans Biography.
  3. Married people—United States Biography.   4. Love—United States.
  I. Stovall, Calvin.   II. Title.
  HQ536.S769   2000
306.81'089'96073—dc21   99-33750
                                          CIP

Book design and composition by L&G McRee
Cover makeup by Lauretta McCoy

AKOMA

THE HEART

Symbol of love, goodwill, patience, faithfulness, fondness, endurance
and consistency. A reference to something loving, not to the physical heart,
but the spiritual heart.

This and the other Adinkra symbols in this book represent images that the Akan people of Ghana, West Africa, have used for thousands of years. The images and explanations of the Adinkra symbols herein are adapted from The Adinkra Dictionary: A Visual Primer on the Language of ADINKRA *by W. Bruce Willis and used with the kind and generous permission of the author and his publishing company, The Pyramid Complex, of Washington, D.C.*

Contents

Libation ix
Gratitude xiii
A Very Special Thanks xvii
Foreword *by Ruby Dee* xix
Introduction 1

The Couples:
A BRIDGE BETWEEN CULTURES: Marcia and David Arunga 5
ON COMMON GROUND: Lateefah Aziz and Steven Gerard-Jones 15
THROUGH THE FIRE: Patricia Blackmon and Brian Foster 25
TOUGH AND TENDER: Sophia and Charles Brewer 35
LIKE I KNOW MY NAME: Girtrude and Charles Browning 47
"DREAM COME TRUE": Pearl Cleage and Zaron W. Burnett, Jr. 55
AN EXQUISITE COMMUNION: Johnnetta B. Cole and Arthur J. Robinson, Jr. 65
THICKER THAN BLOOD: April and Rodgrick Coleman 75
HOLDING FAST TO DREAMS: Rachel and Freddie Cook 85
AFTER THE GAME: Joycelyn and Oliver Elders, Jr. 97
"FOR THE LOVE OF YOU": Inell and Bruce Ellis 109
TURNING POINTS: Louise Goler-Brittain and Harold D. Brittain III 119
RICHES OF THE HEART: Barbara and Earl G. Graves 129
AT THE END OF THE DAY: Alma and Colin Powell 143
A PROMISE MADE, A PROMISE KEPT: Laura Lynem Rates and Norman Rates 151
A PERFECT MATCH: Jane A. Seaberry and Cornelius F. Foote, Jr. 161
TOGETHER IN THE HOUSE AND HOME: Sandra Stevens Jackson and Jesse L. Jackson, Jr. . . .171
TWO LIVES FEED ONE LOVE: Jacci Thompson-Dodd and Mel Dodd 181
WALKING THE WALK: Michele and Richard "Rick" Tingling-Clemmons 193
SOUL CONNECTION: Iyanla Vanzant and Adeyemi Bandele 203

Recommended Reading 215
Permissions 217
About the Authors 219

Libation

We are honoring the Ancestors
We are pouring a Libation
We set a glass of crystal clear water in their honor
We set a small bowl of sweet honey in their honor
and the reason we do this
is that, despite it all,
regardless of what has been said
and shown and misbelieved,
they loved.

Oh yes, they loved
They joined their hearts, their hands, their souls and their flesh
to make marriages and families
They gave birth to their children
who gave birth to more children
who carved the path for us to be here today
and our children to be here tomorrow.

And in that loving and joining and birthing and path-carving,
they found and expressed joy

LIBATION

They made pleasure
They loved fiercely, tenderly, against all odds
no matter how tenuous, risky or painful the circumstances
surrounding those expressions of love, of joy, of togetherness and family.

It is their God-given understanding
of love's impulse
that allows us to exist.

And in honoring one another
through the institution of love and marriage
as expressed in this book,
we honor their memory.

We honor the union of man and woman as an element of nature
and the complementary energy that is the spark of creation.
It gives us the cosmos;
it gives us a spiritual playground
where we can express our love and joy for one another,
our coming together
to continue to create this love
and empower ourselves, our children and our communities.

This is what our Ancestors gave us;
this is their legacy.
Whenever we speak their names in honor,
whenever we pour libations in their names,
we strengthen the bond
that promises our continuity as celebrated through love.

We ask special blessings and protection
for the couples who had the courage to share their stories
and trusted us to tell those stories.
May their love and their marriages continue to flourish and bloom,

may they be safe from harm and disruption,
may the love they share on these pages
be returned to them a thousandfold.

And it is in the name of the Ancestors
and by their grace
that we know the power
and the responsibility of such a gift.
It is in the name of the Ancestors
that we know the wonder of the legacy of their love.

For this, and for all of their blessings, wisdom, guidance and protection
we pay tribute;
we give thanks;
we give love.

This Libation was created with the guidance of Leasa Farrar Fortune.

NSREWA

COWRIES

Cowrie shells are highly polished, brightly colored shells found in warm seas throughout the African continent from western Senegal to Zaire. They symbolize affluence, wealth and sacredness when used by the priests. Dating back to the 1300s, the cowrie was used to purchase food. When the use of currency for money supplanted cowries, the cowrie shell evolved into a symbol of power.

Gratitude

To God, the source of all Life, the cause of all Love, the reason for our Being: thank You for honoring us with this opportunity and providing the means to realize it fully.

To the Ancestors: you are our link to the past, our guardians in the present and our beacons of the future: This one is for you and because of you.

Writing this book took an incredible network of lifelong friends, professional colleagues and first-time contacts who gave selflessly of their time, brainpower, resources and expertise.

Sometimes the words "thank you" are not enough; sometimes they are all you have. We know that you didn't do this for thanks; you did it because you believe in the project and want to contribute a little more love to this world. From the people who jumped on board before there was anything to jump on, to those who kept us on track, steered us over the rough spots and cheered us to the finish line, we offer our deepest gratitude and most heartfelt appreciation. Your contributions provided value beyond measure.

To our parents, Rosalyn Stone, Kathryn Stovall and the late Joe "Simon" Stovall, Jr., and George "Kelly" Stone, for their gifts of life, love, patience and continuing support.

To our agents, Charlotte Sheedy, for believing we had potential, and Neeti Madan, for making it possible for us to realize that potential in this book: your warmth, brilliance, nurturing, common sense and negotiating prowess are the answer to a writer's prayers.

To our editors, Jessica Papin and Diane Stockwell, for sharing and supporting our vision and expertly guiding it through the publishing process: your foresight, enthusiasm and skill were the lights that illuminated this journey.

To our publicist Anita D. Diggs, for so beautifully beating the drum, plucking the grapevine and workin' that spot "by the door": you were the "sign" we prayed for and the blessing that came at just the right time. And to Warner Publishing for having the smarts to put a sistah in the mix: a tip of the hat, a pat on the back and thank you.

To Johnnetta B. Cole and Arthur J. Robinson, Jr., and Jacci Thompson-Dodd and Mel Dodd, for believing in and giving your unquestioning support for this project when it was but a whisper in our minds.

To Pearl Cleage, for leading us to Ruby Dee.

To the "executive committee" who listened, cheered, advised, nurtured, nudged, prayed and propped us up every minute of every incredible day: Michele N-K Collison, Leasa Farrar Fortune, Niki Mitchell, Wanda Lloyd, Doreen Mitchum, Susan D. Newman, Charles Whitaker and Lori Robinson Johnson: you're the best!

To our children, Calvin II and Mariah, for growing so beautifully while Mommy and Daddy were "on deadline."

To the late jazz legend John Coltrane, for the magic of the song, "A Love Supreme," and the inspiration it provides.

The following souls were our "advisory committee" who gave whenever—and often before—we asked. Each and every one of you played a crucial role in pulling this together, and it will take at least the rest of this lifetime to fully express our appreciation.

Bryna L. Bates
Stephanie Berg
Sheila and Rodney Brooks
Angela Browning
Paula Caffey and Celeste Crenshaw
Delmarie Cobb
Evelyn Coleman
Wilbur Colom
Gretchen Cook
Phil Currie
Lara, Shirl and Robert "Dave" Davis
Barbara Eklof
Albert E. Fitzpatrick
Gwen and Ben Floyd
Donna Garland
Kimber Garland
Sitella Glenn
Veta Goler
Patricia Graham Johnson
Della Mae and Rogers Horton
Tracy Horton
Cynthia Kangelaris

Gratitude

Rae Lewis Thornton
Janice Linneman
Lauretta McCoy
Deborah McGee
Jo Moore Stewart
Tamara S. Nash
Kelly Peterson
Susan and Charles Perla
John Pinderhughes
Deborah Posey
Susan Reinhardt
Kirsten Ray
Kathy and Willie Robinson
Charlotte Roy
Carol Saline
Deneice Skaggs
Col. Bill Smullens
The Spelman College Family
Lula Marie Stephenson
Althea S. Stovall
Judy and Anthony Stovall
Stephanie Ann Stovall
Steven D. White
Taryn Williams

The photographers whose works illuminate these pages:
  Dixie D. Vereen
  Nick Arroyo/*Atlanta Journal and Constitution*
  Anthony Barboza
  James D. Coley
  D'Angelo Dixon
  Juan Garcia/*Dallas Morning News*
  Susan J. Ross

Ruby Dee and Ossie Davis

A Very Special Thanks

The response was unanimous: each person who heard we were writing this book asked first thing: "Are Ossie Davis and Ruby Dee going to be in it?"

Everybody knows that you can't even pretend to be writing about Black love without the couple whose very names epitomize all the things that this book is about.

Their fifty-year union, full of passion, creativity, politics and wisdom, is rich and deep enough to fill a book. Indeed, it has. We enjoyed and highly recommend the marvelous *With Ossie & Ruby: In This Life Together.*

So when Ms. Dee explained that they were saving their story for their book and graciously asked whether she could contribute the foreword to this book, we realized we had received a most precious gift.

We thank them for the work they do, the love they share and the example they provide for all of us. To have the gentle jazz of Ruby Dee's words grace this book is a blessing, and we thank her.

Foreword

I used to be suspicious of folks who talked too loud or too long about love. And I must confess that since celebrating our fiftieth wedding anniversary a few months ago and giving birth to a book, Ossie and I have just about overdosed on the topic. I almost don't want to hear another thing I have to say about love and marriage! But then I remind myself that there's no such thing as *too* much love. Not these days. Not when the word itself has almost been relegated to four-letter status. No, this is not the time to jump off the love train. Now, more than ever, we need passion. We need commitment. We need examples. We need survivors. We need *A Love Supreme*.

In your hands you hold a treasure of real-life love stories. Resist the temptation to thumb through to the stories of couples whose names you might recognize. Grab a cup of tea and settle into your favorite spot. This is a cover-to-cover read. Maybe not all at once. You'll want to savor every story. Some will make you laugh; some will move you to tears. All are certain to remind you that marriage is—at its best—a process, a daily vow, an overcoming, a tough gig, a tender treat, an inspiration, an aspiration, a divine pursuit.

Thank you, TaRessa and Calvin, for sweetening the pot! The very next time I'm asked to wax poetic on the subject of love and marriage, I'll be sure to send all seekers in the direction of *A Love Supreme*.

Enjoy!

Ruby Dee

Introduction

Where is the *love* between Black men and women today?

And where are the happily married Black couples?

We rarely, if ever, see realistic depictions of joyous, healthy romance and marriage between Black men and women in the mainstream media or popular culture. And while the Black media—especially magazines and, more recently, films—do a great deal to promote positive images, we are still starving for inspiration, examples and a sense that happily married love is attainable.

Our goal is to reveal one of the best-kept secrets of our time: that, in the midst of racism and other stresses of being Black in America, our men and women are successfully loving one another and surmounting all kinds of hurdles to build strong marriages and families.

We were well into this project when we were reminded of just how urgent the need to share this information has become.

A story on General Colin L. Powell in the June 1997 issue of *Ebony* magazine opens with an anecdote about his wife, Alma, who in her work with young people was talking with an elementary school class about her marriage and family. As she spoke, one little girl raised her hand and asked, "Excuse me, Mrs. Powell, but what does *married* mean?"

That child, in her innocent curiosity, gave voice to a question that many of us are searching our souls—and the world around us—to find the answer to.

Whether we are growing up in or surrounded by single-parent homes, yearning for our own romantic love and commitment or already happily married, we crave images of and information about love that is tender, fulfilling, steadfast and true. We seek inspiration and a sense of possibility; we need proof that there is reason to feel hopeful and optimistic.

The purpose of *A Love Supreme: Real-Life Stories of Black Love* is to spotlight couples whose passion and devotion inspire those around them and offer examples of how sweet, satisfying, challenging and enduring committed love can be. We want to defy the myths and stereotypes that Black men and women are at war with each other and unable to connect in positive, meaningful ways. To show that candlelight, roses, poetry and love songs are an integral part of how we love. And to encourage everyone who is searching for proof that passionate, stable relationships don't have to be an impossible dream.

We chose to celebrate traditionally married couples because, while finding and keeping love is challenging in its own right, crafting a good marriage—even under the best of circumstances—is just plain *tough*. And we wanted to focus on folks who made a binding legal and spiritual pledge to themselves, each other and God to give it their all.

So we embarked on a journey to find couples willing to share their very special love stories and reveal what goes into building a durable, vital partnership based on genuine affection, respect, dedication and trust.

We searched for a varied group, and were astounded by the sheer diversity of what we found. From college campuses to the halls of Congress; from a homeless shelter to a tropical paradise; from corporate boardrooms to international boxing rings; from the country to the suburbs to the heart of the 'hood, we learned that truly great Black couples are *everywhere*.

Most of the folks profiled here are everyday people; some are well-known in their fields, and a few are household names. They are regular folks, role models, ex-convicts, former college presidents, best-selling authors, spiritual leaders, poets, recovered substance abusers, championship athletes and coaches, entrepreneurs, journalists, government workers, top military brass, homemakers, foster parents, elected officials, international and grassroots activists. They range from just makin' it, to comfortably middle-class, to multimillionaires. They are Democrats, womanists, Republicans, leftists, liberals, conservatives and radicals. They express their faith through Christianity, Islam, Buddhism, the Yoruba religion of Ifa and their own spiritual practices. They come from different class backgrounds, cultures, regions and continents. They met each other while growing up, at school, work, church, on blind dates and through wrong numbers.

What makes each couple unique and universal is how, in an age when divorce remains high, they are managing to beat the odds.

We asked each pair how they got together and how they *stay* together. We posed candid questions and got enlightening answers about the passion, romance and friendship along with the conflicts, problems, adjustments and just *plain hard work* that go into building a marriage today.

Although we found no magical formulas, we learned sometimes surprising lessons about what makes their love viable, what makes it "supreme" and what they do to keep it together. And every couple—from newlyweds to those celebrating a half century of wedded bliss— gave us valuable new insights that have helped strengthen our own marriage.

Finally, we wrote *A Love Supreme* to honor the power of a love that brought us from the African continent to every corner of the globe while enduring and transcending the horrors of the Middle Passage, the vile rapes and family destruction of slavery, the chaos and upheaval of Reconstruction and beyond, myths about domineering women and triflin' men and the nonstop messages that we can't/won't/don't love each other as well, as long or as strongly as we should.

This is our way of paying tribute to the strength of spirit and tenacity of heart that led us to jump the broom and forge enduring bonds.

So we invite you to share the treasures that we found on our incredible journey, and to discover some of the many textures, hues and flavors of Blacklove.

TaRessa and Calvin Stovall

MPATAPO

A KNOT OF RECONCILIATION AND HOPE

Representative of a complex knot or a wisdom knot, a bond that is formed after a dispute or a disagreement between two parties. Angry feelings and mistrust may have created angry feelings in both parties. The knot that binds these parties into a harmonious reconciliation represents taking a peaceful approach after strife or disagreement.

Marcia and David with Owuor, Geneiva, Nia and Ebonny

A BRIDGE BETWEEN CULTURES

Marcia and David Arunga
Seattle, Washington, and Nairobi, Kenya

They first exchanged vows in his native Africa and then in her homeland of the USA. They live and work on two continents and are rearing their four children with roots in both worlds. They make the blending of their very different cultures look easy. But Marcia and David Arunga have crossed many bridges and built a few as well to make their marriage and family strong.

David Otieno Arunga, a member of the Luo tribe, was born and reared near Kendu Bay, Kenya, a small town on the shores of Lake Victoria. Marcia D. Tatc hails from a multicultural neighborhood on Seattle's Beacon Hill, not far from Lake Washington.

"Our love is one of the few that I'm aware of that so far has survived the different cultural nuances of the African American and the African African," David says. "We are committed to ensuring that whatever barriers exist are surmounted."

Marcia agrees. "The forging of two people together from two different cultures—who are really one people—that's very important and fundamental to our existence, even though we didn't intend it to be that way."

She didn't know a great deal about African people or culture when she entered the University of Washington in 1977. When they met, David, a junior, was campaigning for student body president and Marcia was running for the Minority Affairs Commission.

Her first impression of the tall, ebony Kenyan was that he was suave and classy, with a smile that went straight to her heart. David was enchanted by the petite, honey-colored dynamo handing out fliers on the campus quad. But their first conversation hit a snag.

"I told her that she was the most beautiful lady I had ever met, and she got very mad at me."

"He told everybody that," Marcia said with a laugh. "There's no woman Dave ever met at that time that he didn't say was 'the most beautiful lady.'"

"I referred to every lady as 'beautiful lady,'" David admits, "but I told her she was the *most* beautiful lady I had ever met."

Though smitten, Marcia told David she wouldn't join his flock of female admirers. But her feelings for him grew. When David was elected the first Black and the first African student body president of the University of Washington, she recalls, "It was my victory, too. I didn't even care that I'd lost."

The first time they were alone together, David told Marcia that he loved her. "It was very fast for me to hear that he loved me. I didn't have

Marcia feeds David a piece of cake at their U.S. wedding.

many boyfriends before that time," said Marcia. "So for this man, who's seven years older than me, to tell me that he loved me, was kind of hard to believe." Still, it didn't scare her away.

Their romance blossomed, interrupted by occasional arguments. A major breakup occurred after the couple argued over Marcia's right to speak during a student meeting about the university ending its investments in South Africa. When she shared her views, David arrogantly ordered her to stop talking. Later in the meeting, she did the same to him. He left the meeting, she followed and he showered her with angry words. Although they no longer considered themselves a couple, they remained friends and eventually patched up things.

"We were always challenged in our relationship, trying to figure out where our boundaries and parameters were," Marcia recalls. "Dave and I argued a lot. I was young. It was my first relationship and I was trying to define who I was as a college student and as a woman. He was older, he was student body president and he was from a culture where men dominate. I was busy trying to gain my own identity separate from Dave's. At the same time, I was attracted to him and wanted to be with him, but not in his shadow. Even when it came to phone calling, I was very old-fashioned: 'You have to call me.' But here was a man who didn't call because he was spoiled by all these women who were running after him. Plus, Dave always said that he was going back home, so 'don't get too close.' Knowing he was leaving, I wasn't sure how much of my heart to put in it."

There was never any question in David's mind that he would return to Kenya. After earning a degree in political science from UW, he worked at various jobs around Seattle, saving for the fare home. His romance with Marcia continued, and she put her cards on the table.

"Ever since I met Dave, I always said, 'Let's get married.' He'd say, 'Let me not cheat you. I cannot marry you. I'm going to go back to my country and I don't want you for a green card; so no! So don't get too attached to me, because I'll be gone.'"

David nods. "You see, at that time most Africans got married to American women because they were under duress financially and they wanted to have a green card. I didn't want to live with that.

"If I were to marry somebody, she had to know where I came from. She had to know who my mother is, who my father is, who my people are. Because sometimes we get married to people on the basis of their being exotic, with African accents, like maybe they're sons and daughters of kings and queens." Marcia had heard of African men who had misled women with made-up tales of royal backgrounds.

Nevertheless, after two years, David had reached the point where he was ready to accept

Marcia's perpetual proposals. "After the fifth time or so, it was kind of like a joke," Marcia says. "He'd say, 'I want to marry you, but before we can be married, you'll have to come and see where I came from and if, after that, you still want to marry me, that is cool.'"

Before Marcia had a chance to visit David's homeland, he asked her father for her hand. The Tate family celebrated with champagne toasts but did not want to lose their daughter to another culture, Marcia recalls.

David returned to Kenya, where, despite his announced engagement to a young American woman, he faced intense pressure to select a local bride. "That he would consider marrying an American woman was a big taboo," Marcia explains. "Not just an American woman, but a non-Luo. My in-laws are sometimes concerned when they talk about other children in the family marrying a non-Luo, even someone from another tribe in Kenya, or even a Luo who's not from their area. There are major family meetings about that. When Dave asked me to marry him, he had to consider that, in his tradition, you are never considered divorced." Even if they divorce and remarry, when the wife dies, her body is shipped back to be buried outside the home that was shared with the first husband.

After Marcia graduated, she became a minority affairs counselor at UW and saved her salary for a trip to Kenya. Then, just before Marcia was slated to leave, she wrote to David saying they should break up forever. The reason, Marcia says, is she felt that "life was changing very fast. At only twenty-one, I didn't know if I was ready to pick up and leave the country, or if I was ready to be tied down. I had really developed my identity and I just got cold feet."

David was devastated. He wanted to see Marcia again, to learn whether they truly had a future. "By this time, I was still of the opinion that she had to come and see for herself if she could feel comfortable fitting into this life. If she didn't feel comfortable with it, I was not going to demand that we be married."

They remained on good terms. "We were friends first, second and always," David says. "Even when we broke up."

In the year that followed, David bowed to tradition and considered becoming engaged to a Kenyan woman, a Luo, like himself.

Then, Marcia wrote to say she was coming to see Kenya, to visit the motherland, which had been a longtime goal of hers. David, who had hosted many friends and colleagues from the United States, let her know that he was looking forward to showing her around. And Marcia wanted to see him—as a friend. When she first saw him at the airport, she was flooded with emotion and the desire to be with him again.

David had instructed his prospective fiancée to make herself scarce during Marcia's visit, and he told Marcia about the woman right away. When the Kenyan woman hung around David's office asking to meet Marcia, he introduced the women, who spent a day together. Later, Marcia told him, "If she was really your type of person, I wouldn't bother to intervene, but I don't think it's a good match."

David searched his soul over whether it was better to marry a woman from his own culture or the outspoken American he could not forget. After acknowledging that their feelings hadn't changed, Marcia and David agreed to marry. But first, Marcia had to meet his family. David's eldest sister, Beldina, served as an interpreter as their parents questioned Marcia about where they would live and whether they would have a lot of children. Her answers—and natural charm—won them over.

Two days later, the bicontinental couple married in a Kenyan courthouse. Their witness was David's eldest brother John, who had seen few African/African American marriages succeed. While John was initially skeptical about the couple's chances of making it work, he became one of Marcia's closest friends.

David was optimistic about his relationship with his new bride. "We had courted over a long period and we knew each other beyond just girlfriend and boyfriend," David says. "I was friends with almost her entire family. I knew that if Marcia could meet my family halfway, then they were not going to have problems with her. I knew that, for all practical purposes, it should work."

Marcia says David warned her that a marriage has to be for keeps, that it was permanent. And they agreed that they would never raise a hand against each other.

Marcia returned home to fulfill her two-year contract as a minority affairs counselor with UW, and David remained in Kenya as the first employee of the newly created agency to develop the Lake Victoria area that was his home. They didn't see each other for nearly a year and a half. In June 1982, David came to Seattle for their formal church wedding, which was held on July 18 at Curry Temple CME (Christian—formerly Colored—Methodist Episcopal) Church.

With both ceremonies complete, David considered whether they should live in the United States, but Marcia wanted to begin their married life in Kenya. "Most of the people I knew who had gotten married in the U.S. took marriage so lightly, it was like there was no chance to be married here. I knew that if we lived in Kenya, we'd have a better chance of staying married because marriage is really important to people there."

While packing to leave Seattle three weeks after the wedding, Marcia learned that she was pregnant. Conditions in Kenya were tense in the wake of an attempted coup. It was a difficult time to be pregnant; she coped with violent morning sickness, culture shock, homesickness and loneliness as David traveled in his work to develop the region. Eventually, Marcia met more people, learned the Luo language and adjusted to the varied rhythms of Kenyan life.

She absorbed the importance of rituals and tradition. "In the village, each time you prepare the food to serve to people, you are more and more a part of the family. As you have children, you become ingrained in the family. Even if Dave and I split, even if I'm not married to him, I'm married to the family. When I die, there's a place for me to be buried in his home. You forge that relationship and it's no longer just me and Dave anymore, it's the two families coming together."

Marcia remembers that it didn't take long for her to feel the embrace of her ancestors' homeland. "The first time I felt I was welcomed in Kenya was at the funeral of my sister-in-law's mother. My sister-in-law's father was crying because his wife had died. Then he looked up and said, 'Who is that?'

"And Dave's relatives, who were still getting to know me, said, 'This is *nyar* Negro—the daughter of the Negroes.' The man stopped his crying and he said, 'Oh, welcome home! Welcome home!' He was so happy that his face lit up. That was the first time I had been really received as somebody who belonged in Kenya."

David later took Marcia to meet an old woman in the hills. "This is my wife," he explained. "She's from America and she's come to live with me here in Africa." When the woman predicted that the American wouldn't make it, Marcia confidently had David translate her reply. "This is my home, my people are from here and I have come back."

In between having four babies, Marcia, a multitalented stage performer, founded the Kisumu Drama Conservatory, where she trained Kenyan children in the theater arts.

She never stopped feeling homesick for Seattle. But when they returned eleven years later, she longed for Kenya as well. "Both places are home. I now come to realize that I'll never, ever really feel comfortable about being away from either place."

Their family business, Seaweed International, bridges the divide. While living in Kisumu, Kenya, Marcia and David sought a way to bring their people and cultures together. Building upon Marcia's interest in fabric and fashion, they founded a factory to manufacture clothes she designed. "This business evolved as a way of developing the economy in Kisumu, giving people jobs, opportunities and some stability," Marcia explains. "We wanted to come up with products that my people, African Americans, would appreciate, so I could share some of the jewels that I'd discovered in my life and time in Africa." When they moved back to Seattle in 1991, they opened Seaweed International, an African clothing store, near Marcia's childhood home.

The striking colors and vibrant designs of the motherland flow from the shop into their home upstairs, where woven clothes and batiks enliven the walls. The Arungas enjoy impromptu family jam sessions and sing-alongs, with other family members sharing African drums and a *nyatiti* (harp) as eldest son Owuor plays jazz/blues trumpet and harmonica.

A bookshelf with photos of extended family members lets everyone know, Marcia says, "that they belong in the house."

The Arunga children, all Kenyan-born, bear names that blend the languages of their ancestry with traditional references to their time of birth: Owuor Obi Otieno, sixteen, is named after his fourth great-grandfather on David's side and Marcia's grandfather, respectively, with the additional name Otieno indicating that he was born at night. The middle name of Ebonny Atieno, fourteen, indicates that she, too, was born at night. Nia, eleven, has a first name meaning "purpose" and a middle name, Akoth, after David's great-grandmother, that means "born during the rainy season." Geneiva Abigail, nine, is named after her maternal and paternal grandmothers, respectively, with the name Achieng meaning "born when the sun was up."

When it comes to child-rearing, "We do everything by seniority; that's an African trait," Marcia explains. "The oldest child gets the first pick of everything, then the next child, then the next. We try to give equally to our children. But that's the pecking order and we're pretty strict with it."

Sharing is emphasized, and when Marcia or David buys the children a treat such as candy or soda pop, they buy a single large serving that is to be divided equally among the children.

"The older you are, the more responsibility you have in the home and to the Luo tradition," Marcia says. Owuor and Ebonny are expected to keep abreast of news in Africa, particularly Kenya, by reading newspapers and talking with their father. They are encouraged to write their Kenyan cousins about family history and current events.

If the family lived in Kenya, Owuor would be building a *simba*, a little house of his own, that would become his ancestral home. Though they are not planning any such formal rites of passage in Seattle, the Arungas work to ensure that their son embodies the best of both African American and African traditions by conducting himself as a gentleman, always careful to honor and respect girls and elders.

Marcia and David acknowledge that in the United States it's hard to maintain the African tradition of having children who are seen and not heard, but they do not allow their off-spring to disrespect adults or address them by their first names.

The Arunga children, typically American in many of their interests, worked hard to shed their Kenyan accents when they arrived in the States. While they fit easily into their culturally diverse neighborhood and schools, their proud bearings and strong home training make them stand out.

During the holidays, the Arungas host and take part in community Kwanzaa celebrations and honor Christmas in the Kenyan way—as a family gathering that emphasizes togetherness rather than gifts or trees. Moreover, in the spirit of Kenya, "where we always had visitors for lunch and dinner," Marcia says, "my home is open to everyone. If they find us at the table, they're welcome to join in." They often eat with their hands rather than forks or spoons, which calls for the Kenyan ritual of some serious premeal hand-washing.

Marcia has mastered the art of making *ugali*, a bread made from white cornmeal in boiling water that is a daily staple among the Luos, though she's just as likely to serve the rice she grew up eating, thanks to her father's Louisiana roots. Collard greens are also a favorite, steamed with onions and tomatoes rather than boiled with pork.

Blending traditions, foods and values seems to come naturally to Marcia, who describes herself as "a Pan-Africanist, a Diaspora person, well aware of Africans living all over the world and adapting to various cultures."

In everything they do, Marcia and David are committed to communicating the truth of African life to Americans. "We always try to share that richness of African culture and diversity of the culture practiced by Africans all around the world," Marcia says. "We want people to know that Africans are not a 'backward' tree-swinging group of people, but people who are very dignified."

These self-styled ambassadors are a study in contrasts. David combines a regal bearing with the deft diplomacy of a natural politician, each word uttered with the richness of an official proclamation. Marcia retains the scene-stealing effervescence of her youthful forays into the performing arts, her observations punctuated by dramatic flourishes and a husky laugh.

They watch each other with subtle affection. "When I look at him and he's not aware, I admire him and I see the part of him that I fell in love with," Marcia says. "But we never do goo-goo eyes together. We don't hold hands. He taught me very early that he doesn't do physical contact in public. It's cultural. And I really resisted that."

"It has nothing to do with my feelings," David explains. "My feelings can be totally different. I may want to be totally animalistic in public."

Their ability to recognize and respect different traditions is central to the strength of their marriage, they agree. Like all couples, however, they have their conflicts. Marcia tries to curb her tendency to erupt in an impassioned barrage of words; David fights the impulse to withdraw into silence. She has learned to wait until he is ready to hear what she has to say. "In a relationship, who wins is not important," David says. "What is important is to carry on."

They take the Kenyan view of marital discord. "It is recognized that families have developed and strengthened through conflict," David explains. "Conflicts have to be resolved on a daily, weekly, monthly and yearly basis, and you cannot spend time looking at conflict as a thing which should draw you apart. Rather, it should draw you closer because you have to be strong for the next day.

"Your success is measured by your ability to stay together through these conflicts. So nobody asks, 'Oh, are you still married to so-and so?' That is not a question. In the U.S., if you tell somebody that you had some conflict, he'll end up suggesting that you get rid of her. In our situation, nobody talks about getting rid of him or her."

Their love, they say, is embedded in their friendship. David explains that the Luo word that translates into friendship is *osiep*—the highest level of commitment between two people. "You can love food or the way somebody dresses or how somebody behaves, but you can't be friends with how somebody behaves or how somebody looks. You can't be friends with food. You can only be friends with the person you have chosen to be your friend. So in terms of a cultural definition of joining together, it is only the word 'friend' that supremely defines what the West defines as 'love.'"

That said, he turns to the woman he describes as his best friend and proclaims, "I love her very much!"

SANKOFA

GO BACK TO FETCH IT

Symbol of the wisdom of learning from the past to build for the future. Sankofa is a constant reminder that past experience must be a guide for the future, to learn from or build on the past.

Steven, Naeesa and Lateefah are united as a family.

ON COMMON GROUND

Lateefah Aziz and Steven Gerard-Jones
St. Louis, Missouri

Lateefah Aziz and Steven Gerard-Jones's interfaith wedding was reported in *Jet* and *Ebony* magazines, and not just because they were well-known entertainment promoters. It seems that the marriage between a lifelong Muslim whose father is the international representative for the Nation of Islam, and an African Methodist Episcopalian with a Southern Baptist background was considered news.

Steve and Lateefah laughingly agree that religion may be the least of their differences.

He's an outgoing, fast-talking promoter—high-powered, hyper-paced and adept at selling his vision to others. She brings a quiet, thoughtful dignity and a passion for details to their professional and personal lives. As partners in Drumbeat International, Steve and Lateefah have provided overseas promotions and public relations along with domestic artist promotions for such talents as Dionne Warwick, Bobbi Humphrey, Public Enemy, Bobby Brown and the late George Howard and Tupac Shakur.

They were introduced at a St. Louis social function in the mid-1980s.

Lateefah admits that when she first saw Steve at the gathering, "he just had this air about him" that attracted her.

Lateefah's sister, Maryum, introduced them. Steve arrogantly asked, "How you doin'?" and, without pausing for an answer, kept walking.

A girlfriend who was with Lateefah and Maryum told them that Steve was in the music/concert business. "Oh, *that's* where he gets his arrogant attitude from," Lateefah said, deciding to forget the attraction.

Fast forward nearly a decade to Chicago's Midway Airport in April 1994. Steve and a friend had just come off the road with an artist's promotional tour and were flying to St. Louis. Lateefah was returning to St. Louis from Ghana, West Africa, by way of Egypt, New York City and Chicago. Both were tired, irritable and running late.

Lateefah and Steven's Christian-Muslim wedding with blessings from (l to r) Khadijah Farrakhan, wife of Nation of Islam leader, Minister Louis Farrakhan, along with Akbar Muhammad, Lateefah's father and international representative for the Nation of Islam, and her mother, Maryam Muhammad

"We got to the gate at about the same time," Steve recalls. "The flight was delayed. I looked at her and said, 'This is not a line or anything, but you look very familiar. Don't I know you from somewhere?'

"And she abruptly responded, *'No!'* I said, 'So it's like that, huh?' Then my partner got into a conversation with her and, listening to them talk, I found that she wasn't really that bad. So I started talking to her. Long story short, we ended up riding back on the plane together and getting to know each other a little better."

Lateefah remembers thinking that Steve looked familiar. "But I'm not the type of person to approach people often. When he asked 'Don't I know you from somewhere?' I thought, 'I can't *believe* he used that old line on me!' I was totally offended and didn't want to have anything else to do with him."

Steve struck out with the second try as well. When they were about to board the plane, he asked Lateefah if she'd like an MC Hammer CD.

"I said, 'Do I look like I listen to MC Hammer?' " she recalls with a laugh. "He said, 'Forget it, then!' and gave the CD to a lady and her teenage daughter, who were also waiting to board the plane. He started talking to them. Watching him interact with the daughter, I saw that he really liked kids. He was really attentive and answered all of her questions." This impressed Lateefah, whose daughter, Naeesa, was about the same age as the girl.

"When we got on the plane, he pointed to the seat across from him and asked, 'Would you like to sit here?' I don't know why I said, 'Okay,' but I did."

It took Steve and Lateefah only a few minutes to realize that Lateefah's sister, Maryum, had introduced them years before.

"I was telling him about Africa and the conversation got pretty interesting," Lateefah says. "He said he wanted to go over there and do some things. I was planning a festival over there and I told him I needed a group." By the time the plane landed in St. Louis, Steve had asked Lateefah for her phone number.

It took Steve a while to make the call. "I had this policy where, if I met a girl and I liked her, I didn't call right away. If you call too soon, they'll think you're desperate or bored." After a round of phone tag with each other's answering machines, they connected.

"I said, 'This is Steve.' She said, 'I know who this is.' Later, I found out she claimed I talked too much," he says.

"I'm the quiet type, and he just dominated the conversation," she explains.

They started seeing each other as friends and soon they were hanging out every day and eating dinner together. "She was the last person I talked to at night, the first person I talked to in the morning," Steve says. "We would get into deep, deep conversations. We had something different to discuss every day."

And sometimes to debate.

One of their first was about Marcus Garvey, the Jamaican-born Black nationalist who worked to organize a back-to-Africa migration in 1920s Harlem.

"I'm not going back to Africa," Steve insisted. "I feel like our people built this country, brick by brick, and I'm not going anywhere!"

"This is not your home," Lateefah countered.

Eventually, they agreed to disagree.

They also asked about each other's faith. "I was kind of confused about the Muslim religion, I didn't know what it was all about," Steve says. "Like many people, I didn't realize what a common faith it is among Blacks in Africa. I thought it was about Black separatists. I didn't realize that it was as powerful as it is. I had seen this as a Christian world, because I grew up in a Christian society."

He had to confront his own stereotypes as well. "When you hear about Muslims, if you don't know better, you think they're all radicals because you only hear about them when things are being blown up. I thought they were separatists who went around hating White people.

"Later, I found out that it wasn't about that. I've always respected Minister Louis Farrakhan and the things he spoke of, but I didn't realize how real those things were."

On visits to Steve's AME (African Methodist Episcopalian) church, Lateefah discovered "many similarities between the Bible and the Holy Qur'an. But I'm still getting used to the singing and shouting . . . because to me there's so much noise and so much going on," she says.

The exposure to Steve's religion is "making me a more well-rounded person. And that's what I'm really looking for, for myself and my daughter, Naeesa."

Steve helped Lateefah get a musical act for the festival she was coordinating in Ghana. When she was there for the festival, she "missed talking to him every day, missed his sense of humor, his jokes."

After eight months of friendship, the feeling was mutual. "Whether she knew it or not, she had become a confidante to me," Steve says. "I'm an extremely private person. Being in the entertainment business, I watch people's personal lives get raked over the coals and spread to the whole world, and my true personal life is so valuable to me. It was the first time I had had someone I could say anything I felt to, without feeling restricted or like it would be spread all over town."

Steve found Lateefah a welcome contrast to "the typical video girls that you meet in the entertainment industry, who don't care anything about you as a person. They just want to get into the Grammy after-party or the American Music Awards," he says. "Here was a woman who had been associating with the presidents, kings and queens of countries and she wasn't hung up on that type of thing.

"She was somebody who genuinely cared about how I felt. Sometimes when people ask, 'How is your day?' that's just a figure of speech. But when Lateefah asks, it's genuine; she really wants to know.

"I'm constantly stressed out, and early in the relationship, she said I needed to take time out and she paid for me to go to a masseuse. That was the most caring gift I'd ever received. Nobody had ever given me something just for *me*, just to help me feel better."

Their memories differ on who was the first to acknowledge that their friendship was becoming much more. Steve recalls that, while helping Lateefah hang some blinds at her mother's house, she said, "You know what? I think I'm falling in love with you."

Lateefah remembers saying it, "but that was *after* he said it to me! After I got back from Ghana, one night we were talking on the phone—"

"No, no, no, no, I have to clarify that," Steve chimes in. "Right before I hung up, I said, 'I love you.' And she was like, *'Please!'* And I said, 'No, don't misinterpret this. I don't mean love in the sense of birds chirping and harps. I love you and I want to be around you and I want to be with you, as more than just a friend. Don't think that I'm head-over-heels and all that stuff. I don't know you well enough to be *in love* with you. I love you, but I'm not in love.'"

"When he said that, I felt that he did love me, but—that man thang again—he didn't want to admit it, so I admitted it first," Lateefah says. "But he just threw it out there to see what was going to happen."

How did Steve respond to Lateefah's declaration?

"Suddenly I felt like I was about twelve years old. I automatically started searching my soul, trying to figure out whether I felt the same way about her, asking myself, 'What does she mean by that?'"

When he asked, she replied, "I mean what I just said."

"Once she broke the ice by saying, 'I love you,' I felt more comfortable," Steve says. "It took a long time to meet someone like her."

After that conversation, they started holding hands and discussing more personal matters, including their goals for the future. "We just started talking more about things that we wanted to do, how we could benefit each other and how we were going to do things together," Lateefah says.

"And then we began to dream more with each other, to talk about our future," Steve adds. They went from "me" and "I" to "us" and "we," becoming more of a team.

"I felt Lateefah was a true partner that I could bounce business ideas off of, who had similar goals," Steve says. "Once we joined arms, we never skipped a beat."

He didn't have any qualms about marrying a woman who had a child, and enjoys a close, honest relationship with Naeesa, fourteen, a budding ice skater, whom he describes as a "good kid, extremely gifted and intelligent."

"I asked Naeesa how she felt about the fact that her mom and I were getting pretty serious," Steve recalls. "I explained that it was important that she and I like each other. To love the tree, you have to love its branches."

"With it being just me and my mother for so long, it was a little strange having to share her with someone else," Naeesa says. "Their announcement of marriage didn't come as much of a surprise, since they had been dating for a while. I had come to know Steve and he spent a lot of time with me. We became good friends. I'm glad my mom and I found someone like Steve to share our lives with."

And Steve, who is a "surrogate father" to his eighteen-year-old nephew Christopher, says, "I feel God's really blessed me with everything I ever asked for."

Steve asked Lateefah's father for her hand in marriage and proposed to her at a party on New Year's Eve 1995. After she said yes, he proposed to Naeesa.

Lateefah's parents took the couple's religious difference in stride. "Growing up, my parents always stressed the importance of having God in the center of your life. I believe they would have preferred that their daughters marry someone of Islamic faith. However, as long as the person had a strong belief in God, it was fine," she explains.

Steve and Lateefah had discussed how they would handle conflict, housework, cooking and chores.

"Whoever gets home first starts dinner," Steve says. "It's not a matter of men's work or women's work."

He admits that Lateefah demolished his stereotypical view of Muslim women as docile and passive. "Even though she's quiet, she has guts. She's extremely strong and assertive. She stands on what she believes in, and backs it up."

Their union was reported in the February 1997 issue of *Ebony* under the headline "Weddings of the Year."

Naeesa confers with Steven and Lateefah during an ice skating session

Lateefah and Steve find common ground in their belief in God and areas such as mutual respect. The Holy Qur'an and the Bible, they say, share several family values with which they both agree. Unlike many contemporary couples, they kept the word "obey" in their wedding vows. "A lot of people take 'obey' out of the vows," Lateefah says, "but we both said that we would love, honor and obey each other. It's obeying each other's wishes and obeying the will of God and the sanctity of the marriage."

As different as their temperaments are, living and working together doesn't create friction. They enjoy each other's company, share jokes and balance each other's personalities. "I'm high-strung, juiced, ready to roll," Steve says. Besides keeping him calm, Lateefah knows how to cross the *t*'s, dot the *i*'s and separate the real from the fake.

Perhaps most unique to Steve is the honesty they share. "I can say what I feel, she can say what she feels."

When they do argue, "We have huge blowouts, like a huge storm," Steve says. "But just like a storm, it goes right out the same way it came in. And it's never forever; I don't think we've ever been mad at each other over a day."

Confiding that Steve is "the biggest practical joker," Lateefah says they laugh a lot at work and at home. "I think we were just meant for each other," Lateefah says with a smile. "It just clicked for both of us. I like him to be around. We don't have any major, major differences. And he encourages me to reach out and do the things that I want to do. He listens to my side, tells me I can do it and just makes me feel good about myself."

To keep it real, she says that "we always agreed that, whatever the feeling, we would bring it out in the light, discuss it and get it over with, for good or for bad."

"Everything that was missing is now here," Steve says. "It's total fulfillment, like the missing piece of a puzzle. I want us to go down in history as having one of the greatest loves—ever."

On Sunday, April 11, 1999, Steven Gerard-Jones passed away from an aortic aneurysm.

"Putting my husband of two years and six months—almost to the day—to rest was the hardest thing that I have ever had to do," Lateefah says. "I lost my husband, my best friend, my life partner and my soulmate. A very close friend of the family, whom I consider my second father, told me to 'think of Steve as a gift from God, borrowed to give me

the greatest happiness and joy I have ever known. But then, just like all things borrowed, it has to be returned to its owner.'

"So I can't ask 'why?' but only say 'thank you' for allowing me that time I had with him. I guess his wish of having one of the greatest loves ever has come true."

AKOMA NTOASO

THE JOINED OR UNITED HEARTS

A symbol of agreement, togetherness and unity in thought and in deed.

Patricia and Brian at their Valentine wedding

THROUGH THE FIRE

Patricia Blackmon and Brian Foster
Asheville, North Carolina

Patricia Blackmon and Brian Foster's 1996 Valentine's Day wedding in an Asheville, North Carolina, homeless shelter was not the ceremony they had envisioned. But after a very long engagement, during which they'd been to hell and back, it was, in many ways, more than they had hoped for.

Though their hearts were joined from the beginning, it took them nearly two decades to formalize their union. Brian proposed to Pat on the night they met. He promised to pay for her divorce from the husband she saw sporadically and swore he'd take care of her.

"The first night I met him, I knew I wanted to be with him," Pat says. "I told him that I felt the same thing that he felt. For seventeen years, he asked me to marry him. For seventeen years, I told him I would—when I was ready."

It was the summer of 1979 at the newly opened Krispy Kreme doughnut shop on Patton Street in Asheville, a small mountaintop town possessed of both beauty and charm. Pat, who was the first Black person hired to work there, staffed the drive-through window. Brian and a car full of friends pulled up to the window.

Brian asked her name and if she was married. "Yeah, but I'm separated," she replied. He started to pull away from the drive-through window, but couldn't leave. He left the car with his buddies and went inside. "Next thing I know, he was sitting at the counter," Pat recalls. "He's a shy person, but he was bold that night."

"It was love at first sight," Brian explains. "I said, 'She's gonna be mine.'"

Brian stayed until Pat got off work at seven o'clock the next morning. They sat on a hill

Brian and Pat enjoy a postwedding limousine ride.

overlooking Asheville and got to know each other. She was twenty-seven, married to a man who she says abused and abandoned her, and the mother of an eleven-year-old son. He was a twenty-two-year-old forklift driver who liked to party and run with his friends.

She liked his honesty. According to Pat, she felt "relaxed, real safe and secure just talking to him. I never felt like that with another man."

Pat had been committed to making her marriage work, though her husband had been living in Virginia for five of the six years of their marriage. Occasionally, he stopped by for a visit, expecting to find Pat waiting. She was.

But meeting Brian had her in a spin. "I felt the chemistry when he pulled up to the window. I was feeling something I'd never felt before, and I was afraid 'cause I was a married woman." Moreover, despite her husband's absence, "I cared about him. I believed in my vows. I believed in marriage. I was sad, because I felt like I wanted to be with Brian but I couldn't because I was already married. I had to do the best I could to make that marriage work, whatever I had to take to do that. Not getting involved with anybody else was one of those things."

For several months, Pat fought her attraction to Brian. When he called, she asked for more time to sort out things.

In the middle of her husband's next visit, Pat realized she'd had enough. She finally gathered the strength to leave him for Brian, who told his friends that he would be spending his time at home with Pat and they wouldn't be seeing much of him for a while.

When Pat stopped by her house to pick up some belongings, her husband showed up. "He wanted to get violent," Pat says. She left the house and called Brian, who came to get her. She stayed away from the house for a few weeks, until her husband called from Virginia and said she could have her divorce.

Pat and Brian had been together for months before they became intimate. "He asked me, and I kept tellin' him, 'No, I can't right now. When I'm ready, you will know.' And it took me that long to get comfortable mentally and physically."

He was happy to wait.

Pat filed for divorce. Brian pressed for marriage. Pat begged for time. When the divorce became final two years later, Brian asked what was taking her so long. "I was tryin' to heal myself from a real messed-up situation. I wasn't sure I wanted to get married, but I was sure I wanted to be with him."

She had a lot of heartache to overcome. Her son, Alan, had been born when Pat was sixteen. The daughter she'd had with her husband died at age five. Her husband's infidelities and long absences left deep psychological scars. His hands, she says, had inflicted beatings, a broken jaw and knife and gunshot wounds.

"In my body, my mind, my heart and everything, I was still tryin' to recuperate," Pat says.

In the meantime, Brian was there, steadily saying he loved her, steadily asking when they could get married. He promised he'd never let anybody hurt Pat. She believed that he was sincere, and assured him that they'd marry when the time was right. But first Brian had to work through some issues of his own.

"I was young and wild. I liked to hang out with the boys and at that time I was drinkin' and smokin' pot," Brian says. "He grew up drinkin'," says Pat, who never drank or smoked until she was twenty-three.

Then there were the women.

Pat says he chased them.

Brian says *they* were chasing him.

Pat had to cope. "It took him a while to be honest. That was one of the reasons we did not get married. I had to have total honesty. He was a good person. He had a good heart. He had very good intentions. But he had to deal with the other women. I told him, 'If it's going to take us twenty years to get married, I'm still here. I'm not going nowhere.'"

She knew he had a lot of growing up to do. "I was waiting on him to find himself, totally and completely. I wanted to be there with him to do that, but not *married*. When I met him, he asked to marry me; he said he loved me and would take care of me. And I felt he meant that. But you have to do things for yourself, too.

"Him and the fellas liked to go out of town and party and stay gone. I wasn't going to go through that for another man."

Eventually, Brian quit hanging as much with the fellas and stopped worrying about being called "henpecked." "I've never loved anybody else," Brian insists. "Not like this. I would rather be with her, anywhere she wanted to be."

Brian had won awards as a cosmetologist and wanted to work in that field again, but he kept his forklift driving job so he could take care of Pat. She appreciated Brian's sentiments, but says she is "too independent" to sit at home being taken care of. She left Krispy Kreme for a job at the Department of Social Services and dreamed of someday owning a clothing boutique.

There was another hurdle for Pat and Brian to overcome. Although he functioned well and worked steadily, Brian was still drinking and smoking marijuana. After snorting cocaine a few times, he learned to cook it up for smoking. He got so good at it that, according to Pat, "he became the 'lab technician' of Asheville, with clients from Florida, New York and Washington."

As drugs became more central to Brian's life, Pat, who rarely drank or used drugs, slowly joined him. "I wanted to be a part of what was going on. It was lonely. I didn't want to feel like an outsider, sitting by myself while a bunch of people partied."

Getting high made her feel insecure and defensive. She had started using drugs to feel more involved and included in Brian's world. "After a while, I just felt like maybe if I had this in my hands, in my reach, I'd have what it took to make him happy." Instead, Pat says, "the drugs were taking him farther and farther away from me."

As a dealer, Brian spent increasing time in the streets and more nights away from home. The lonelier she became, the deeper Pat sank into the drug lifestyle. Like Brian, she'd become a functional drug abuser. For nearly four years, she got high, went to work at the Department of Social Services, came home for a lunchtime hit and returned to the office. Then she'd come home and "get right back into it." Eventually she began selling drugs.

Essentially, Pat explains, "Drugs proved to be more powerful than me. Like people say, it's mind over matter. It takes your mind. So it doesn't matter."

She tried giving Brian an ultimatum: her or the drugs. Then she asked him to at least do his business at home, instead of in the streets. She even packed his belongings just to let him know that she was serious. Nothing changed.

"I cared about him and I knew he cared about me. I knew that this man had made me happy. It's just that I had to be patient enough for him to overcome everything that was goin' on in his life. When he was able to deal with it, I had to let him deal with it the way he could, not the way I wanted him to deal with it. I couldn't come first until he was ready for me to come first. He *said* I was first, but let it be known that the drugs were first."

Eventually, Pat lost her job, and the couple lost their apartment. Police suspected them of dealing, but had a hard time catching them. Their luck ran out when, in the midst of a drug raid, Pat was caught holding a $10 rock—Brian's "rainy day" stash. Pat did twenty-four days and Brian twenty-seven in the Buncombe County Jail. It was the longest they had ever been apart.

They resisted the police's attempts to turn them into informants. But, jobless, homeless and behind bars, they knew that something had to change.

Salvation came in the form of a representative from the Asheville Buncombe Community Christian Homeless Shelter, who visited Pat in jail. She was told she had two choices: to get out of jail and do what she'd been doing; or to go to the Ash Brook County Christian Ministry (ABCCM) shelter, where someone would help her get her life together.

Pat reached a turning point. "I had never been in trouble a day in my life. Here I was, in my forties and in jail. I lost a home and a job; I lost everybody. One piece of rock which you paid ten dollars for on a street cost me about three thousand. It wasn't worth it. Eventually, you've got to make a change for yourself and want it for yourself."

Incarceration wasn't new to Brian. At age sixteen, he'd spent two days in jail for stealing tools from a business. This time, police said, he might do forty years of hard time. "I saw the light," he says. "I saw I was headed in the wrong direction. I said, 'I'm not going to prison.'"

"I had to do the right thing. I wanted to make it better for Pat. I wanted to make it better for myself." He told Pat he'd never again put her in the position to go to jail "behind any stupid stuff."

When Brian was released, he went to the ABCCM shelter "to go find my baby." The shelter was out of room, so Brian slept on the porch. Soon a space opened up, and together the longtime lovers began working to kick the habit that had caused their lives to crumble.

They started working at the shelter: Pat as a resident assistant and Brian driving the shelter van. He got into playing the church piano on Sunday mornings. They lived apart, in dorm-like rooms, conforming to the shelter rules, giving their all to the process of recovery.

"I told him that this was one thing I could not do for the both of us," Pat says. "It was hard enough doing it for myself. This is something that he had to want himself. Not because of me. Not to keep me."

Brian reached deep within and found the strength to battle his longtime addictions. For the first time in his adult life, he was completely clean and sober.

When they had been at ABCCM nearly a year, shelter manager Donna Wilson told Brian that, when the time was right, she would pay for them to get married at the shelter. Brian rushed to propose to Pat—on one knee.

"Tears just started coming out of my eyes," Pat recalls. "He said, 'Is that a yes or a no?' I said, 'It's a yes!' I had always dreamed that. I never expected him to do anything like that. It was like a fairy-tale dream come true.

"He said, 'Good things come to those who wait.' And I felt like I was waiting for something worthwhile."

Their wedding ceremony transformed the shelter into a romantic haven, where they were surrounded by the people who had witnessed and supported their struggle back to wholeness.

After a honeymoon in Asheville, Pat and Brian pointed out a log cabin on a hill that they had admired. "We both looked at it and said, 'Boy, it sure would be nice if we could live there.' Back at the shelter, Sam, an employee, said, 'I have a surprise for you. How would you like to live in the log cabin? This is a wedding present,' and handed us the keys."

"I said, 'Thank you! How did you know? Do you have a pipeline into the Lord?'" Pat says with a laugh.

Reflecting upon their wedding, the years that led up to it, as well as the challenges ahead, Pat and Brian realize there are no shortcuts to happy endings. "We are still traveling." Pat sighs. "It's a long haul. It's still got bumps and ruts—"

"But we've been straight ever since," Brian interjects.

"And we talk about it, too," Pat continues. "About the drug thing. I make him promise me that if he's using them, please tell me. That's all I want. I want to be able to have honesty in the relationship, to communicate with each other. If we don't, it's not going to work."

In times of trouble, they feel the true force of their bond. "When she's hurt, I hurt," Brian says. "I can feel somethin' wrong with her. Even if I'm not around and somethin' happens to Pat, I can feel it."

Once, Pat was robbed on the job and locked in a cooler. Another time, she got stranded on the highway. Both times, Brian appeared unexpectedly, saying, "I felt like somethin' was wrong with you."

Although they disagree on many things, they don't stay mad for long. "After about ten minutes, we make up. I apologize, say I know I was wrong," says Brian. "Then she says the same thing. That's what keeps us together, I think. Because we're mostly honest with each other."

"Whenever we have differences, we don't go to sleep, no matter how late it is. We talk about it and get it out in the open," Pat says.

"That's what keeps us strong," Brian adds.

The only thing Brian worries about, he says, is Pat—where she is, how she's feeling, what's going on with her.

Pat says she worries "about everything—whether I'll be able to fix a meal for him that he wants to eat, whether I'm going to have what I want to wear to work tomorrow, about the bills next month, whether I'm going to be able to live comfortably or not."

Until recently, she worried about Brian's drug and alcohol abuse.

Brian says that while his love for Pat has always been strong, he let drugs interfere with their relationship because he was "young and weak-minded." Now that they're clean, the relationship is better. "We get to laugh and enjoy ourselves more. We're not ashamed to go out in public."

"We're not vampires," Pat says. "We can go out in the daytime. We can go to the movies or get ice-cream cones. With drugs, we didn't go nowhere. We only left the house to get more drugs. Now we both looked forward to going to work."

"I like being happy all the time," Brian says. "Being able to talk to my family and her family. When I was on drugs, I wouldn't even look at anybody. I love it now. I didn't know life could be like this."

"It's strange," Pat says, "because he's clean and he's more aware of a lot of stuff that I tried to get him to be more aware of when he was usin'. He watches old movies, romantic movies, a lot of comedy and horror. He goes and buys me movies now. He's even brought books home. He shares the cookin' now, where before I couldn't even get him to go in there and boil water. Now he'll cook for me."

She says it was hard for her to get used to "because I was used to doin' all this myself. Now he says, 'Let me do this,' or it's done before I can get to it."

Without drugs, Pat says, "I love him more. I'm ready to give him all the love I was givin' coke."

That's not the only change. "Now that I'm her husband, I see myself differently," Brian says. "My feelings for Pat are stronger. I care more about her than I ever did before. I can't do the things I used to do—the way I used to talk to other women. I can't hang out like I used to. I love being married. I feel more responsible. It makes me feel good. Feel like I'm important now."

What gives him the faith and confidence that he can stay clean? "Pat. I turn to her when

I'm not feeling strong, and she'll say, 'Come here, let's talk.' She's a rock. If it wasn't for Pat, I wouldn't have made it."

They know their upward climb is far from over, and the demons of the past must continually be kept at bay. "It's not gonna be smooth going no matter how many years we're together." Pat sighs, a shimmer of vulnerability in her large, expressive eyes. But, as she looks at Brian, the light of determination shines through.

After all these years, Brian says, "I still haven't figured out what makes her special. She's just different. When she talks, I have to listen because she makes sense."

As Brian coaxes a haunting melody from a piano in the shelter, Pat affirms that their present, past and future are marked by a bond that was formed long before they exchanged rings and vows. "He can make me happy; he can make me sad. He can lift me up; he can tear me down. We've been homeless together. Hungry together. Cold together. Sick together. On drugs together. Locked up together. In recovery together. He's never left. He's never once left."

FAFANTO

THE BUTTERFLY

A symbol of tenderness, gentleness, honesty and fragility. A related proverb says, "The butterfly may be fluttering around a pot of palm wine, but will not drink it for it cannot afford to buy."

Sophia and Charles at their wedding

TOUGH AND TENDER

Sophia and Charles Brewer
Pennsauken, New Jersey, and Philadelphia, Pennsylvania

After scoring eight straight knockout victories, Charles J. Brewer got coldcocked in the first round of a 1994 fight. When his fiancée, Sophia Boyd, saw him fall, she stopped cheering and started praying.

She was pregnant with their first child and worried that Charles wasn't going to get up. For the first time, she tasted fear and had a change of heart about his boxing career.

"I hated boxing. I used to cry and think, 'Maybe he'll hurt himself and he can't box.'"

But the sight of the formerly invincible Charles lying helpless on the canvas changed all that. "I never had a fight scare me so bad. I went over to the ring and he looked *through* me. I could see him, but he really couldn't see me. He was so shaken up. I thought, 'This could be really scary. He could really get killed.'

"I realized that it was no joke; it was serious business and he was actually risking his life every time he stepped in that ring. When he was winning, I thought, 'Oh, it's not that hard, just throwing a couple of punches, knocking the guys out.' But when I saw him hit the canvas and I didn't know if he was gonna get back up, I just prayed.

"All those bad things that I used to wish, I took all of that back. I said, 'One day he might not get up off that canvas.' I support him a lot more now than I used to," Sophia admits. Although she still resents the forced separations of his prefight training regimen, seeing Charles knocked out changed her tune to, "If you're gonna train, make sure you train *right*."

After that loss, Charles fought his way to the United States Super Middleweight Championship in 1996, and the International Boxing Federation Super Middleweight Championship Title in June 1997. Unlike many young fighters, for whom boxing is the best ticket out of rough beginnings, Charles, a twenty-nine-year-old computer consultant and budding entrepreneur, boxes simply for the love of the sport.

As committed as he is to fisticuffs, his greatest passion is his wife and their growing family. Whether teasing Sophia about how he ignores her advice, describing the antics of their four-year-old son, Charles, Jr. (a.k.a. "Bam Bam"), or doting over their baby daughter, Jasmine, the intense, chiseled young man known in his training gym as "The Hatchet" is all proud chuckles and tender glances.

This young couple conveys the comfortable fit of a much older pair. As his lovely, doe-eyed wife snuggles against his shoulder with a contented smile, Charles praises her ongoing support and the sacrifices she makes for his boxing career. Sophia describes her growth in a voice that combines youthful delight, business savvy and homegirl sass.

"I support him a lot more than I used to. Before, I had some selfish ways; it was all about me. I realized that this is about us, because we're a team. When he's in training, when he's fighting, it's hard for him and he needs my support. Now it's like, this is *our* life, our thing."

They met as teens in their north Philadelphia neighborhood. She was fourteen, with strict, super-protective parents. He was eighteen, "with a street vibe, tryin' to get her attention."

As Sophia walked home from school, Charles moved in for the mack. "What's your name? How you doin'?" Sophia ignored him. "I didn't have the time for him and he was like, 'What's your problem—stuck on yourself or somethin'?' He harassed me every day."

She took his number when he offered, but didn't use it until she'd done her research. "I didn't know him. I knew his sister, Olivia. I wanted to know what kind of person he was, and asked around. I heard he was a good guy; he had graduated from Roman Catholic [high school]. I said, 'Okay, he's all right.' "

They started out talking as friends, then one day Sophia realized, "I like this guy. I had to keep him a secret for a little while. I couldn't really let my mom know [his age]. When I told her I liked him, she asked me how old he was. I said, 'Oh, he's seventeen.' He was almost nineteen then. I couldn't tell her 'cause I knew she was gonna go crazy."

For the first year, Charles walked Sophia home from school, dropping her at the corner to avoid parental suspicion. Charles's mother, while not as strict as Sophia's, "didn't exactly approve of my having somebody that much younger than me," Charles remembers. "She knew that Sophia was still in school and she was pushing for her to finish school before anything started between us."

They talked on the phone (though Sophia had an iron-clad eight o'clock phone curfew) and saw each other secretly. Once Sophia's mother realized the young sweethearts were still together, she made it a point to meet

Charles "Bam Bam" Jr.

Charles kisses Jasmine.

Charles's parents. "She didn't say, 'You can't see him,'" Sophia says, "but she was concerned 'cause she wanted me to finish school. She didn't want him to sidetrack me.

"But he wasn't that type of person. He would encourage me to do what I had to, and that was good. My mom realized that I was gonna see him, so she'd say, 'Well, maybe Fridays or Saturdays, he can come over and spend a little time with you while I'm here to supervise.' "

Despite all the rules and regulations, Charles stuck with Sophia. While he appreciated her good looks, he was drawn to something more. "A lot of guys don't want to go with the girls in the neighborhood, and vice versa," he says, because they were familiar with each other's ways. Charles was one of those who swore he wouldn't date close to home. "But she seemed a bit different. She didn't hang out in the street, so I had never seen her outside with the crowd, running around. She had good principles. I didn't have to worry about somebody else coming up to me and saying, 'Man, you been with *her*? Guess what she did!' "

Charles was Sophia's first "real"

The winning belt—and fist—of a championship fighter

boyfriend. "He would just make me laugh so hard. And while I was around him, he made me feel happy and so complete. His [childhood] nickname was 'Boo.' I used to wonder, 'What is it about Boo that I like so much?'

"When I saw him, I got butterflies. When he wasn't there, I missed him. He would bring me flowers and teddy bears; he just always made me feel like I was special. Other guys tried it, but it wasn't like Boo. You hear about all the games, but he was very sincere. When I needed him, he was there. He took me to my prom; we went to the movies. We were inseparable."

The same quiet confidence and air of ambition that attracted Charles alienated Sophia from the local girls. "The females always said, 'She thinks she's better; she thinks she's cute,' " Sophia remembers in a voice tinged with echoes of loneliness. "I couldn't go outside without having a confrontation with somebody. I never thought I was better than anyone. I just thought that I could have a lot more out of life and I felt they could, too. It's like, 'You don't know me, you're just judging me because I choose not to do some of the things that I think are wrong. Because you do it, I don't say you're no good. I just say I know you could do better.'

"To this day, they still don't like me. I grew up with them. They used to play with me when we were little. Now they see me and they turn their heads, and it makes me feel bad because they really don't know what kind of person I am. They never gave me the opportunity to let them see who I really was."

Recently, Sophia was pleasantly surprised when one of the neighborhood girls who hadn't spoken to her for a long time "came over and told me that she wished she would have stayed in school and done some of the things I did. She told me that she was really proud of me, and she said, 'They don't like you because you're doing something with yourself.' "

Fortunately, peer rejection didn't dampen Sophia's ambition to do well in school, or her goal of becoming a beautician. After high school, Sophia opted for beauty school over college. By the time she earned her license, "I knew I wanted to be a shop owner."

Meanwhile, Charles, who had been boxing since childhood, dreamed of a career in the ring. Even in his early teens, it was evident that he had the drive to train, the heart to win and the moves to take him to the top. When he was a skinny eight-year-old being tormented by neighborhood bullies, Charles's mother signed him up for self-defense classes. Boxing was one of the activities offered. "When I was around twelve, I started liking it a lot," he says. At fourteen, he began working with his trainer (and now co-manager), Bobby "Boogaloo"

Watts, who was one of the leading middleweights in the world in the 1970s. Charles recalls that when he started coming home with "busted lips and black eyes," his mother said, "Wait a minute. I only took you there to learn how to fight. I didn't expect you to *like* this."

Nevertheless, he stuck with it, and when Bobby suggested going pro, Charles gave it serious consideration. He trusted Bobby's judgment and together they worked toward that goal.

During their courtship, Sophia didn't think much of Charles's boxing. "I wasn't impressed," she says. "I thought, 'Oh, he's a boxer'; it didn't matter to me. It really started to matter when it took time from us. Then I hated it. 'I have to train, I can't hang out. We can't go to the movies tonight; I'm tired,' he'd say. I used to cry." And secretly hope that an injury would end his interfering career.

Despite the separations his regimen imposed, they never dated other people or broke up. In addition, Charles found another passion. After working in a retail job at a Pep Boys auto store in the 1990s, he spent some time in the corporate office, where he was introduced to computers. Fascinated by the technology—and liking the fact that the guys in corporate dressed better and made more money than their colleagues in retail—Charles set his sights on a job in management information systems. He went to computer operations school, where he was a top student, and took his newfound knowledge to Pep Boys' corporate offices.

He was making pretty good money. One night while they were out to dinner, he asked Sophia what she thought about moving in together. She told him that she was willing, but her mom would say, "Why buy the cow when you can get the milk for free?"

On Christmas Day 1993, Charles joined Sophia's family for the holiday. He was wearing a suit and looking good, Sophia says. "Then he gave me the ring and I opened it and that's when he asked me, in front of my whole family, to marry him. I was really shocked and scared and crying. My grandmother was crying. I said yes."

In April 1994, they moved in together; in September, Charles, Jr., was born; and on June 17, 1995, they had a big wedding at Wayland Temple Baptist Church in Philadelphia. And Sophia saw a new side of Charles.

"He's the type of person that doesn't show any type of emotion. But that day, he seemed like the happiest man. I was happy, but I was really nervous. He was grabbing me, hugging me; he was just so loving, he made my day! He made it seem just like a fairy-tale wedding."

Their Happily Ever After had its challenges. Being married and a mother at twenty-one years old "was hard," Sophia says. "I loved my baby, but I didn't know if I was ready . . . being so young. I had all these responsibilities. Every time I had a problem, I would say, 'Mom, what should I do?' I really didn't know, and I wanted to be a good mother; I wanted to support Charles and not nag him, 'cause I'm used to having my way.

"My mom said, 'You have to grow up. You wanted this, you wanted to be with him. You're gonna have to be in his corner. Some things he's gonna do that might not be right, but you're gonna have to let him be a man.' " Sophia says she is learning to listen more, refraining from nagging and accepting that Charles does things in his own way and time.

Charles has had to adjust to his changing relationship with his childhood homies. "I knew them before I knew her," he says. "As we grew older, all of us went our separate ways eventually, but growing up . . . if you had a buddy that you were used to rolling with every day and all of a sudden you're like, 'Well, I'm gonna be with Sophia, man,' they're asking, 'What's wrong with this guy?' They had their problems with it."

"There have been people around us that did not like our relationship and they pulled at it, but it seems like the more they pulled, we pulled together," Sophia remarks.

Although Charles's heart is firmly rooted in north Philly, he has realized that he can't hang out with his old friends. "I'm not the same. No matter how much I want to be with them, be like them, they won't allow me to be. Because they see the money, I've got a certain status, they won't let me be myself."

Still, Charles refuses to let go of his Philly roots. While they bought a home in Pennsauken, New Jersey, a Philadelphia suburb, "I'm urban," he states proudly. "I don't care if I end up on [Hollywood's] Rodeo Drive; north Philly will always be my home." His city-based training gym, their longtime church and their new hair salon attest to that bond.

Straddling different worlds seems to come easily to Charles. He left Pep Boys to work with Judge Technical Services, a computer consulting firm. He appreciates the steady income, the chance to work in a challenging and satisfying field and the option of having an income once he gives up boxing. His "day job" also provides a contrast to the blood, sweat and fears of pro boxing.

Just as computer consulting won't distract Charles from boxing, he doesn't take his athletic persona to work. "When I'm at work, people in the corporate world don't understand at all how I do what I do. They and the people I grew up with both say, 'You can switch back and forth so good.' I can be talking to a VP in a certain way, and turn right around and talk to my buddy in another way. They say, 'I don't know how you can do that.'" But Charles enjoys being part of "a well-rounded circle of people." He draws a definite line, however, between his careers. He often has to remind his work colleagues that, "when I'm at work, I don't want to hear about boxing. I don't want to talk about boxing. See what's on that computer screen? That's what I'm focusing on right now.' And when I'm at the gym, I don't want to talk about work. I just click like that. A lot of people don't understand."

Boxing is a way for Charles to express his emotions. When he started boxing, his father acknowledged Charles's accomplishments, but was clearly not impressed. That just made Charles work harder. Any anger, disappointment or frustration he feels simply fuels his fists. "I love when stuff gets on my nerves. I just hold it in; I hold a lot of stuff in. When I get to the gym, I take it out on them."

Boxing is also an outlet for his greatest sorrow. The death of his beloved mother shortly after Charles, Jr., was born "sucked everything out of me. I've never gotten over it. I don't like to talk about it. It makes me angry; it makes me sad." His voice is tight as he shares this, and his muscles seem to clench with the painful memory. Losing his mother took the shine off his greatest boxing victory. The night he won the championship, he told an interviewer that "as happy as I am, and with everything that I feel I've accomplished, I would trade all the fanfare and glory [of the title] to have my mother back."

As he changes the subject to boxing, Charles exudes the coiled energy of a jungle predator. The edges of his face and body seem to harden and his eyes show a laser glint as he tells how his first loss brought out his killer instinct. "I was very, very angry. I didn't know what was going on. I was undefeated for fourteen fights. I was on a high." The media had anointed him "Charles Brewer, up-and-comer, hot prospect," he says. "Right after the articles, I was given a loss—I didn't lose, but the judges voted that way—and all of a sudden, things changed." Now, he says, he leaves nothing to chance and goes for a knockout every time.

The right preparation is essential, and Charles trains for several weeks before each fight. He moves into a hotel for the duration, and even if he stays near home, he can't see Sophia or the kids or speak more than a few words to them. "I'm away from home. My coach and trainer take me completely away from everybody. It drives me crazy sometimes. The way I set my mind is that I don't want to talk to my family. If I start talking to them one day, I'm gonna talk to them the next day. Then I'm gonna want to go see them, and you can't do that because it will break your concentration." And that leads to problems in the ring.

"So the best thing to do is call and say, 'You'll see me in the ring and I'm all yours when this fight is over with, but for the time being, I've got to take care of business. I've got to keep my mind set on one thing.'" He admits that the separation takes a toll on him and Sophia and causes tension between them at times.

Sophia agrees. "It's hard because sometimes I want my husband," she says, her tone plaintive. "He's in the city, but I can't call him. I can't come see him. Sometimes I feel it's unfair to our marriage. I might really need him, but I have to sacrifice my needs."

Charles offers another view. "You only have me to worry about. But I've got so much stuff. I've got the media pounding on me; they want to see everything I'm doing. I've got all these eyes watching me. Everybody wants to talk to me, and all the while I'm tryin' to keep my mind set on my fight."

Charles made an exception and trained from home in April and May 1999 when Sophia was expecting their second child. The fight was scheduled for May 12 in Germany, and Charles worried that the baby would be born while he was away. Happily, he was in the delivery room when their daughter, Jasmine, was born on April 28. Two weeks later, with Sophia and the children at home, Charles won the fight in Germany with a TKO in the second round.

While training time is often lonely, fight night is a whirlwind of emotions. Sophia has been to nearly all of Charles's fights. But it doesn't get easier. "I really haven't adjusted; it's hard," she admits. "I pray all the time. I sit in the front row. My heart is beating. I'm very nervous. My mom and I usually go together, and before he goes into the ring I'm just so *nervous*, running into the bathroom, wondering 'What's gonna happen? Is he going to get hurt? Oh, Lord, please let everything be all right. I'm so scared. . . .' It's like my heart is gonna fall out.

"Once he gets in that ring and starts throwing leather, I calm down. I'm into it then and I'm calling to him, 'Boo! Knock him out!'"

In the ring, Charles is oblivious. "To tell the truth, when I'm fighting, I don't even see her. I could be looking dead at you and I wouldn't even see you. I can't be thinkin' about how you're feeling; that's a distraction."

When the fight is over, Sophia still has to wait to get close to Charles. With people and media all around him, she can't touch or talk to him until he comes home. Then he's all hers until the next round of training begins.

Like any couple, they engage in emotional sparring. Sophia says she used to tell Charles what to do, "trying to be a second mother to him, like he's not raised." Her mother advised her to support Charles. "And that's exactly what I did. I must say it was hard for me. But I loved him so much that I felt that if we're going to have bad times, we're just going to have bad times together. I always thought that we could work through it. It took a while, but we did."

They argue "a little bit," Sophia says, "but it's nothing to the extreme." They handle conflict in very different ways. "If she's upset about something, she doesn't care where I am," Charles says. "It's like, 'I want to talk to you *right now!* '"

"He'll let me talk, and he'll just sit there," Sophia retorts. "He won't say anything. He stores anger; I want to get it out." Nevertheless, she's heeding her mother's advice and learning that it's best to wait until she cools down and Charles is ready to listen before beginning a discussion.

Though he gives her a hard time, Charles admits that "sometimes I'm the type of person that needs to be put in his place, 'cause if I had somebody who just did whatever I said, I probably couldn't deal with that. But she would *never* let that happen. She'd say, 'Wait a minute, buddy. I don't care who you are, you're not gonna [treat me] like that!' "

"We're still learning, but we know we have to communicate," Sophia says. "I know that, as a woman, I have to let the man be the man. I wanted to be the woman and the man; I liked to be in control. My being so bossy can kind of push us apart. So I have to take a different approach to how I handle things. Even though I think I might see things that he can't see, sometimes I have to lay back and let him see things for himself."

When someone—such as his father or Sophia—suggests a course of action, "I never do it at the time that you tell me," Charles says. "I'll wait and wait and wait."

Later, when they're talking about something else, he'll tell Sophia, "You were right about what you said last week, but . . ."

"We can laugh about it," Sophia says with a smile. "We'll just talk about what he did last week when he ignored me and I was mad at the moment, but I'll look back and say, 'I *was* goin' off on you, wasn't I?' So it makes us grow."

Beneath Charles's tough-guy exterior lurks a stone romantic. He buys Sophia clothes and jewels and surprises her with sexy getaways. "But I'm not gonna woo you with words," he says. "What you see is what you get." When she jokes that he doesn't buy her roses often enough, he tells her to look at her diamond earrings. Ultimately, he confesses, "There's nothing I wouldn't do for her. She's my guardian. It's like I have another set of eyes and ears; somebody I can trust in. I think I need her more now than I needed her before. Because, for one, I'm in the public eye and there are a lot of things that happen so fast. So it helps to have a person in your corner, giving support. And I think we complement each other. In the areas where I'm weak, she's strong, and where she's weak, I'm strong."

Seated in their newly renovated unisex hair salon, Round One Impressions in Philadelphia, Sophia and Charles are embarking upon a longtime dream. Giving his wife the opportunity to run her own shop "was one of the things I always wanted to do," says Charles. "I don't know anything about hair, but I know how to run this business, how to market it and how to get people in here."

Sharing a grin, the Beauty and the Boxer silently agree that they make a knockout team.

OSRAM NE NSOROMA

THE MOON AND THE STAR

A symbol of faithfulness, fondness, harmony, benevolence, love, loyalty and femininity. The moon, which often symbolizes femininity, receives its radiance from the sun, so therefore it is dependent on the sun. To the Akan people, this interconnectedness symbolizes the interdependence of man and woman in marriage. This mutual cooperation between the two individuals is the essence and the foundation of their success in marriage.

(From left:) Jade Bolton, matron of honor; daughter Kelley Hicks, flower girl; Girtrude; Charles; and John Browning, Charles' brother and best man

LIKE I KNOW MY NAME

Girtrude and Charles Browning
Little Rock, Arkansas

Charles Browning gave Girtrude Hicks his telephone number and she threw it away. Twice.

But it wouldn't stay gone.

He noticed Girtrude on his route as a mail carrier. He complimented her beautiful smile, and asked if she was married.

"Sort of," she told him. "It's on the edge."

"If you need somebody to talk to, call me," Charles said, handing her his number.

"I stuffed it in my pocket," Girtrude remembers. "When I got home, I threw it in the trash. When the kids emptied the trash, the phone number stayed in the bottom of the trash can. A day or two later, I got the number and threw it away again. After the garbage man picked up the trash, I got the water hose to wash the can out and there's the number. It kept showing up, so finally I went ahead and said, 'Let me call. . . .' "

"Hey, Girt," Charles said, recognizing her voice instantly.

Charles was divorced and rearing his sons, Carlos, eleven, and Charlie, nine, alone.

Girtrude, an elementary school secretary who was getting divorced at the time, was a

47

single parent to Aundria, thirteen, twins Candece and Bryan, eleven, Kelley, six, and Robert, four.

Single for six years, Charles says he had become frustrated with the "phony" women he was dating. "They wanted somebody to take care of their bills. Before you sat down and got to know each other good, it was, 'My lights got turned off; I need some money to help me get 'em back on.' I didn't mind helping. It was just, 'Is this all you want me to do? What is the relationship based on?' It wasn't based on us getting to know each other or wanting to be friends."

Charles "had a strange feeling" about Girtrude when they met. "It wasn't the same as with other women. She played kind of hard to get and never mentioned anything about money to me at all. I admired how she was handling those five children by herself. She wasn't saying, 'I need a man to help me with these kids.' I saw how we could be friends."

Their friendship took root quickly. After surviving violently abusive first marriages, both had dedicated themselves to Christ. "We'd both had really bad deals, and it was comforting to be with him because he knew what I was going through," Girtrude says. "We enjoyed each other's company and didn't want anything from each other." They went to Bible Study together, shared recipes and meals and organized activities such as at-home pizza-and-video-viewing parties with all of the children. The whole group attended church together, too. The children got along "surprisingly good," Charles says with a smile.

Though he felt an "awesome connection" with Girtrude and was impressed with her youthful glamour, maturity and patience amid the ruckus of five children, Charles wanted to just date rather than marry.

Others suspected what the couple themselves did not see. When Girtrude told her mother that Charles was "just a real good friend; he's not looking for a wife or anything," her mother said, "Fool, you can't see the forest for the trees."

As Girtrude and Charles fell in love, they felt guilty about having a relationship out of wedlock. But Charles balked at making a deeper commitment.

"I was scared. Because, in my last marriage, my ex-wife tried to kill me."

His ex was a "street woman," Charles says, who drank and used drugs. "I thought I could get her and change her into what I wanted, but it didn't work that way. I was seeking the Lord, but her pull was so strong that I fell in with her. I became what she wanted. I just drank and drank and drank and even got into drugs."

They were splitting up when Charles's ex, who he says was using crack cocaine, convinced him to give her a ride in his car. "On the way back, she came out of nowhere with a knife and stabbed me in the neck and chest. I felt myself dying. I just cried out to the Lord."

A nearby policeman called an ambulance to take Charles to the hospital. Once recovered, he started seeing his ex again until a friend warned him, "You're goin' down next time." Charles realized, "That was enough for me right there."

Girtrude had spent years in "a very abusive relationship with my ex-husband, thinking it would get better, and it didn't. I almost got killed and went through some really trying, hard times.

"My parents had been married fifty years and we were raised where you didn't divorce your husband. You stayed there. My mom's philosophy was, 'Everybody's got some kind of problem; you've got to put up with some.' I left home and graduated early at sixteen, and the next year I was married and started having babies. So I left my daddy's home, went to my ex-husband's home and never experienced adult life on my own. When my ex told me, 'You've got a pretty face, but that's all, nobody's gonna want you with five kids,' I believed it and stayed a lot longer than I should have."

Once free from the confines of her marriage, Girtrude wanted to have some fun and do a little traveling, which she did while relatives watched the kids. Charles, who says he had "trouble staying with any woman," never thought he'd be married again. "But the power of love is amazing. It'll change your mind," he says.

After he and Girtrude became engaged, Charles's family and friends "started influencing me. They said, 'She's got five kids and all she wants you to do is take care of her children. If you buy one pair of jeans, you've got to buy five.' "

Girtrude tried to convince Charles that "if the two of us brought our families together and both of us had made a decision to work for the Lord, that union would only bring about a greater good. We'll do better together than we could do apart."

Charles, however, listened to the naysayers and broke their engagement. But that didn't give him any peace. He missed Girtrude so much he couldn't sleep at night. "I was dreaming about her, wondering what she was doing. So I'd get up and drive by her house. It got ridiculous. I prayed to the Lord, 'Whatever You say.' And my spirit said, 'I want to be with her, nobody else.' "

In November 1990, two days after the breakup with Charles, Girtrude was diagnosed with cancer of the throat. "Charles didn't know any of this. I went ahead with the surgery [to remove the cancerous cells], not knowing how traumatic it was going to be."

During her six-week recovery, Girtrude "prayed and prayed and prayed. 'Lord, I'm alone and You told me that this was my husband. I believe it like I know my name. I just want to know what happened. If this *is* my husband, I want him to come by. I just want You to send him.' "

One Sunday, while her children were at church with her sister, Girtrude was praying when the doorbell rang. Charles walked in. "I asked him why he came by and he said, 'I don't know. I had to come.' "

Charles cried when he learned about Girtrude's cancer and surgery. "He said he was so sorry, he just didn't know what to do. But he knew that I was supposed to be his wife."

They had a small church wedding on July 3, 1991, with Girtrude's youngest daughter, Kelley, as the flower girl. As part of the ceremony, the pastor "called all the children together and united us as a family."

While the couple had overcome their own hurdles to marry, getting the children on board was a challenge. The two oldest—Charles's son Carlos and Girtrude's daughter Aundria, both teens—had the biggest adjustments to make.

Like many single parents, both Charles and Girtrude had unconsciously made their eldest children their surrogate emotional partners. "We had both been very unfair with them," Girtrude reflects. "Because, through no fault of her own, I made my oldest daughter like my spouse. She helped me make decisions; she knew what bills I had to pay. She would help me with those younger children; they would obey her like they would me. I did that to her; I really leaned on her.

"And the same with Charles and Carlos. He rode in the other seat in the truck, alongside his father. Charles talked things over with him . . . and now, both kids saw somebody moving in."

"It was a war with us and them," Charles recalls. "Her daughter was working on me and my son was working on her, trying to play two ends against the middle. So Girt and I joined forces and we watched each other's backs."

The younger children weren't as hard to win over. But even in tough times, Girtrude and Charles "tried to stay real honest. We never said 'your kids' or 'my kids,' " Girtrude says. "It was always 'the kids.' When mine would try to call Charles 'Stepdad,' he'd say, 'No, your real Dad stepped out. I'm your Dad. *I'm here.*' "

Grandparents presented another challenge. Charles's mom considered Girtrude too strict, while Girtrude's mom didn't think Charles should discipline her granddaughters.

"I said, 'Well, Mom, they eat Charles's dinner, they go in Charles's refrigerator, they turn Charles's lights on, they run his water and use his phone. I think he's in a position to offer a little discipline.' "

According to Girtrude, they manage discipline by presenting a united front. "Even if I don't agree with the way he disciplines at that particular time, the children never know that. I back him up one hundred percent before the children." Any differences are discussed behind closed doors.

"Our biggest challenge has been the children," Girtrude says. Despite the hurdles, she and Charles have "high hopes" that all of the children will do well and be successful. The couple's commitment to nondenominational Christianity has helped them gain spiritual insights and turn his-and-her children into a true family.

"We didn't get an opportunity to instill some of the things in the older kids that we've been able to instill in the two youngest ones, Robert and Kelley," Girtrude says. "I just feel like we had a second chance with the last two. And then the Lord has a way of almost stopping time for you and giving you another chance with the older ones as well." They are pleased to report that former coconspirators Aundria and Carlos have grown into hardworking, successful young adults. And eighteen-year-old Bryan has accepted a calling as a youth minister.

The strong religious practice that has helped the Brownings to overcome abuse, sidestep death and replace fear with faith is a cornerstone of their union as well. A few years after marrying, they became nondenominational evangelistic ministers. "It's a nontraditional approach toward getting out the gospel of Jesus Christ," Girtrude says. "We're more charismatic than traditional preachers. We believe in speaking in other tongues, the laying on of hands and in the baptism of the Holy Spirit."

"We believe in walking in the example of Jesus Christ," Charles adds. "We believe in the whole Bible, the Old Testament and the New Testament." Charles ministers to youth in detention homes, talking with, rather than preaching to, young male sex offenders. He and Girtrude minister to inmates in state prison as well as to married couples and newly blended families, openly sharing the lessons from their own life struggles. Girtrude also works with single mothers, sharing the lessons she learned when she was in their position.

And as they minister and teach, they continue to learn. Girtrude says, "I have grown so much spiritually with my husband. We're faith people; we believe that every day is going to get better. As far as our marriage is concerned, I don't think either one of us had any idea that it was going to be that way.

"We're really united in most areas because I know that Charles is going to give the response that's coming from the Word and I'm going to do the same thing. So you won't get two stories or two sets of advice from us. I just don't know if we could do it any other way."

As ministers, Charles says, "We complement each other because she can put my thoughts into words. I don't know how she does it, but I can tell her something I want to minister on, just kind of speak my thoughts, and she can take and run it down and be very articulate. . . ."

"Because we are ministers, especially a couple ministering together, there's always someone trying to break us up," Charles says. "You have to fight for your marriage."

Which they're both ready and willing to do. "We don't quit," Girtrude says. "We don't give up. We don't burn out. We just go back, regroup and get a new strategy."

"Our minds kind of roll the same way," Charles says. "I might say, 'The Lord told me to bless a certain person,' and she'll say, 'He told me the same thing.' We pray together, we touch hands and agree on most things."

After so many ups and downs, Girtrude says that now she is at peace. "This man married me and I had five children. It's really a good marriage. I didn't have to settle for anything. I didn't have to lower my standards, and they were pretty high."

In the midst of guiding seven children to adulthood and ministering to troubled souls, Girtrude and Charles never lose sight of what they cherish about each other.

"What I love about Girt is she's so understanding, sensitive and real attentive to what makes me happy. She'll do things like take my shoes off, wash my feet, lotion them down and massage them. She's smart and we can talk and talk about anything."

The woman who tried to trash Charles's phone number, then prayed to God to send him back through her door, views her sweetheart through admiring eyes. "I don't think there's been a time when I wished that we had made other choices. Charles is probably one of the most genuine people I've ever known. What you see is what you get. He doesn't hide his wit. I appreciate him just being himself. He's a giver and he often thinks about what he can do, how he can be a blessing to somebody else. That goes way past me and our children. The needs of other people are just a high priority with him."

Giving thanks for their God's grace, Girtrude and Charles exude contentment with each other and this juncture of their lives. He balances the stresses of delivering mail with the challenges and satisfactions of ministering; she gets satisfaction from both her religious outreach and her work as personnel manager at the state's information technology agency. They've recently moved into a house with ample room for the whole family, bought Charles a new truck and welcomed three grandbabies into the fold.

The Brownings of Little Rock, Arkansas, just want to testify about the miraculous power of love.

GYE NYAME

'TIS ONLY GOD

A symbol of the omnipotence, omnipresence and immortality of God,
it refers principally to the greatness of God and reflects God's power
over all of His creation.

Pearl and Zaron laughing all the way to the altar

"DREAM COME TRUE"

Pearl Cleage and Zaron W. Burnett, Jr.
Atlanta, Georgia

"Monogamy is the death of love," the free-spirited Pearl declared.

Zaron was cool with that.

He read the books that inspired her, and they discussed each one. As partners in running Atlanta's venerable Just Us Theater Company, they poured their life experiences and philosophies onto the stage. They wrote, produced and performed their avant-garde theater pieces in the Club Zebra Floating Speakeasy. Through their plays, they spoke openly to their audiences about love, relationships, their fantasies and their pasts. About social/sexual/political issues and personal solutions. About the ways that love and freedom intersect, collide and, occasionally, merge. They shared secrets, dreams, opinions and revelations with friends, strangers and fans. They basked in the applause, then stayed to clean up the performing space after the show.

Their friendship began in the 1970s when they were married to other people and had children to raise. They worked side by side in Atlanta politics, divorced their spouses and later gave in to a force that seemed to pull them together.

"The feeling that has always attracted me to her is that it's like I don't feel like I have a choice," Zaron (known as Zeke) says. "Most people I could take or leave, but with Pearl, I never felt like I had that option."

"We felt like we met each other in the middle of a conversation that we didn't get through with last time, in whatever ancient place we were in . . ." Pearl muses.

"Probably some slave ship action," Zeke exclaims.

They slip into an imaginary exchange from a past-life rendezvous:

"Where are they taking you?" Zeke asks.

"I didn't get to ask you what do you think about God," Pearl cries. "Oh, you're not going to South Carolina, are you?"

"I'm going to New Orleans."

"Oh, gosh," she frets, "I won't see you no more, right?"

Zeke shakes his head, locks flying. "I hope to see you on the other side."

In the 1980s, they worked together for Pearl's ex-husband, Michael Lomax, as he campaigned for and won a seat on the Fulton County Board of Commissioners.

"Once Zeke and I really got to know each other, then it was clear to me that I wanted him to be a person who was close to me," Pearl says. When they first met, "I was married and working on a million things, so I wasn't thinking about how we could be together. But he was such a good person to me. For me it wasn't saying, 'Okay, this has to be the person I spend the rest of my life with.' It's, 'Okay, this is somebody who's going to be close to me for the rest of my life.' "

For his part, Zeke "wasn't unhappily married. I had children . . . at the same time, there's another part of you that is focused on something else. It's not that you're working towards it. It just is. You can't deny something that is. You can try to pretend it's not and all that kind of stuff, but that drives you crazy. It wasn't like I was trying to figure out a way to do anything."

After their respective divorces, their friendship ripened. "I believed that we were moving from being friends into being something else," Pearl remembers, "but at that time I was completely opposed to marriage. I felt that monogamous relationships were the death of love and that was the most ridiculous decision you could possibly make.

"I was a newly minted feminist, so I had book theory. I had everything about why women should not take any guff off of men. I was a new revolutionary. So I had no qualms about saying, 'You're absolutely wrong. You don't know anything about this. Yes, I think a lot of stuff about you is really perfect, except you're a rabid chauvinist and you have a huge gap in your education because you've never read these books.' He was annoyed that I would challenge him, but he was the only man I knew who would read everything I was reading, so then we could talk about it without my having to force the issue."

The first book that Pearl wrote, *Mad at Miles,* contains a chapter called "The Good Brother Blues," which says, in part:

> *I think it is time we put forward a working definition of* who *and* what *we are looking for. We are looking for a good brother . . .*
>
> *A good father/good husband/good lover/good worker/good warrior/serious revolutionary righteous brother . . .*
>
> *A love black women, protect black children and never hit a woman righteous brother.*
>
> *A brother who can* listen. *A brother who can* teach. *A brother who can* change. *For the better . . .*
>
> *A brother who doesn't hit or holler or shoot or stab or grab or shove or kick or shake or slap or punch women or children . . .*
>
> *A brother who knows there is no such thing as a rape joke.*
>
> *A brother who knows that time and tenderness are more important than size and speed and that reciprocity is everything.*

Pearl realized that she had found all that—and more—in the cocoa-colored self-proclaimed "emperor" who challenged her beliefs about nonmonogamous love.

"He really appealed to me as an artist and a writer. He did all the stuff that I thought was really exciting and manly. He was strong, fearless, political but really funny. I've had relationships that were really rich and wonderful and I wouldn't trade them, but there is always a point where the person kind of looks at you and says, 'Oh, my God, this is a wild woman!' But with Zeke, we keep turning to each other and the other one is always like, 'What else? Whatever it is you're going to do, just do that.' So it's that kind of permission to be yourself—it's wonderful.

"You know somebody who is free and likes you to be free, who is not trying to say, 'Don't do this!' and 'Don't do that!' or 'Be this!' or 'Be that!' But just the fact that we could be free together and be a man and a woman, that we could also be lovers, that we could also be intimate physically was like, what more could you possibly want?"

Zeke's description of Nina Mae Little, the lead female character in his novel *The Carthaginian Honor Society*, reads like it just may have been inspired by his vision of Pearl:

> *Nina Mae Little was the type of woman who can land anywhere on the face of the Earth and be greeted by smiles and offers of assistance. . . . She was a fine, mid-forties Black woman who became more completely beautiful every day. Not in the traditional way most Americans mean, that is, younger by the day. Nina Mae looked every day of her age, and wore them with the ease of one born to be beautiful from the cradle to the grave. Her smile was unearthly in its absolute dedication to mirth and sincerity. . . . The crustiest of white Southern politicos had been known to melt when in her company . . . women appreciated Nina Mae, men adored her, and young people believed her to be sent from Heaven above.*

Zeke and Pearl moved in together, in a cozy corner house in southwest Atlanta, where she lives upstairs amid Black female images and energy and he resides downstairs in a more masculine lair, complete with weight-lifting equipment and a big-screen TV. Where each is allowed the space for self-expression without the compromise of more traditional households. Where they call each other on the phone to make dates and set up rendezvous. Where, as Zeke says, they stay sane because they haven't tried to merge their lifestyles.

Though comfortable with the notion of commitment, Zeke had his own reservations about matrimony. "Here in America marriage as an institution is confused with marriage as a concept. Marriage as an institution comes with definitions and expectations that some partners never discuss with each other. Thus, what starts out as an unscripted adventure becomes a very contrived pursuit of a certain type of lifestyle. Marriage as a concept is a real sweet idea, with two people looking at each other and saying, 'I really think everything I want to do on this earth I'll be able to do better with you as a partner,' which is a step beyond, 'Why don't we start living together for life?' "

He understood the rationale of nonmonogamy. But his heart had a logic of its own. "I really can't imagine a more complete fit, so I'm not even looking. I don't have any more interest in wasting any of my time looking for somebody else. I found exactly what I'm looking for. Do you agree? And if you agree, well, let's not look at nothing else and put all that time that we would have been looking doing stuff together, which you can't do if you're not willing to make that commitment."

As to the big M, Zeke says, "I made it clear that I would be open to the question."

Pearl tiptoed toward marriage with "very little steps because I fell in love in a very different kind of way. It wasn't that I had to take a position on it, it wasn't like I had another political decision to make, it was just that I couldn't imagine being with anybody but him."

Then she had a revelation at thirty thousand feet. "I was on a trip . . . either coming

Pearl and Zaron at Atlanta's West End Performing Arts Center

back from New York or someplace. We had been living together and everything was cool. I felt really lucky and grateful that we had found each other. I remember looking out the window of this airplane at all these wonderful clouds and the sky was blue and it just felt perfect and it was like those moments when you hear a voice say, 'I think we should get married.' So I went home and said, 'I'm so glad I'm not dead. I love you! Let's get married. . . .'

"He did the wise thing. Knowing that I hate to fly and had been drinking vodka on the plane, he said, 'Let's wait until morning and if you still feel this way, then we can deal with this.' "

"So we woke up in the morning and I said, 'I think we should do it.' "

They immediately sent out invitations to a wedding celebration scheduled for May 1, 1994, but found they couldn't wait. So on March 23 they invited a judge friend to officiate, a musician friend to play the saxophone and about twenty-five loved ones to share their celebration. The ceremony was as spontaneous as a performance at Club Zebra. Candles illuminated the house. The judge, Clarence Cooper, came on the way home from work. Saxophonist Joe Jennings got the invitation while resting from an exhausting road trip. When he heard who was getting married, Jennings said, "Oh, Lord, let me get my horn," and set the tone for the wedding by blowing "My One and Only Love."

"It was a perfect wedding because there were only people here that I absolutely loved, and everybody was really glad that we were together and that we were so happy together," Pearl recalls.

Their creative endeavors enrich their relationship. While putting together some new theater pieces for Club Zebra, Pearl and Zeke still join forces for projects such as the screenplay version of his novel *The Carthaginian Honor Society.* Artistic vision pushes both to write across boundaries. "I write novels, Pearl writes plays and we collaborate on screenplays and performances. I'll write a play and she'll write a novel, but I'm a novelist and she's a playwright and then we come together on the other stuff."

When Pearl's first novel, *What Looks Like Crazy on an Ordinary Day,* became one of Oprah Winfrey's book club picks and a best-seller, Zeke was as proud as he could be.

They don't read or critique each other's work while it's in progress, but share it when it's ready and offer support.

They continue to work through such issues as his tendency to break objects when angry, her impulse to cry in the face of conflict, what to do when words no longer work. He lifts weights, plays golf and watches gangster movies. She reads Buddhist literature "because I love the point of view" and clears her mind to sift through what to let go of and what to keep.

The important thing, they agree, is that they don't pretend there is nothing wrong. When problems arise, they confront them head-on, even when it's painful.

One of their biggest conflicts took place in 1992. They were living and working together, struggling to keep their theater company alive. Pearl received a commission to write a play, *Flyin' West,* for Atlanta's large, prestigious Alliance Theater, a mostly White institution where longtime friend Kenny Leon was making his mark as a brilliant young Black artistic director.

Zeke announced that he could not attend the play's opening with Pearl because it would be "a betrayal" to their work. Viewing it as a threat to the viability of their own theatrical endeavors, he suspected her of "leaving a distressed ship, one that was low on fuel, to go to a big White company just for money."

Pearl, who had earned her college degree in playwriting, explained that she was weary of wearing so many hats for Just Us/Club Zebra. She helped Zeke to see that her opportunity at the Alliance wasn't about the money, but because she craved "a chance to work just as the playwright, not to have to also raise the money, take the tickets at the door, clean the bathroom, make the costumes . . . but just to be the playwright. I was going to take that chance." They talked until they'd expressed their feelings and each understood the other's point of view. Then Zeke happily escorted his wife to the opening night performance.

"We didn't walk away," Zeke says. "We had gone through so much. Just having rules for discussing hard stuff. It's a lot of work to get to that point, but it's worth every bit of it because unless you do all the work, you won't appreciate the moments of sweetness."

Marriage, rather than being "the death of love," has changed their relationship for the better. "I could not have imaged being closer. . . . It's like a completeness," Zeke says. "It's a really wonderful feeling to know that no matter where you are on earth, there's somebody else who's thinking about you, whether you are in their presence or three thousand miles away."

"I think it's better, it's sweeter," Pearl says with a smile, "to know that there is another person who knows you absolutely, who you can trust. There's nothing that I wouldn't tell him; there is no subterfuge. There's just a complete feeling of love and acceptance, to know that someone really does love you specifically not because you have this kind of eyes or this kind of hair or you work here or you've got this, but it's somebody loving what you love about yourself."

If there is a sound track for their love story, it would include the Temptations, whom Zeke pays tribute to in his essays and performance pieces. "Their style is what I grew up on in Detroit," Pearl says. "The first little 45 record I ever bought was 'Dream Come True' by the Temptations. I remember hearing that record as a girl and saying, 'When I fall in love, I want somebody to feel about me just the way this song feels.' So when I started knowing Zeke, he acted like the Temptations sounded."

Like a man who was reared to love and respect women. A man whose father took his four sons to pick violets for their mother. A man whose great-great-grandfather, after the Civil War, traveled the South to free his wife and all his sisters from the various plantations they'd been sold to. A man, Zeke says, from a family in which "there are other family members who worked all day and then had to walk six miles at night to go visit their girlfriends and come back home and be at work at six the next morning. In our family, it wasn't unusual to sacrifice for love. In fact, it was expected. If it wasn't somebody you were willing to walk six miles each way for at night, every night, then don't talk to me about *love*, it was just somebody you liked a lot."

Pearl admits that she steals the things Zeke says for her plays. "All the cool guys in my plays get to say these lines. They turn to the women and say something so loving and wonderful and cool that you can hear women sigh in the audience."

They all have a little of Zeke in them?

"All the good ones do," Pearl confesses, a grin crossing her luminous face, a fan in her hand fluttering with the coy finesse of a Southern femme fatale.

Zeke responds with a nod of contentment. Sparks of sensual energy dance in the air between them. "Nothing is better than being in love," he says. "The rest of that . . . don't mean nothing. I've had everything I could possibly have. I've had money. I've not had money. I've had everything and the only thing I know about any of it is that I'd rather be in love."

As for Pearl's earlier philosophy, she says, "When I was in my 'monogamy is the death of love' phase, I tried to make the case for this with my older sister, who is only and has always been in love with the one man she is and has been married to. So she laughed at me like, 'This is a phase my little sister is going through about this monogamy.'

"I said, 'Why do you find that so funny?' And she said, 'Because there's a level of intimacy that you can't have unless you are committed to somebody, living with them, married to them.' So I, of course, being the baby sister, said 'Yeah, she *thinks* she knows. I'm more modern. I understand about these things.' "

Flashing a quick smile, Pearl gazes at Zeke and says, "And she's absolutely correct. She was completely right. Which I told her. I called her and said, 'Okay, I was wrong and you were right. Thank you for telling me, and it's true, it's really *true*.' "

ANANSE NTONTAN

THE SPIDER'S WEB

A symbol of wisdom, craftiness, creativity and the complexities of life. To the Akan people, this small insect demonstrates how individuals can ingeniously use their resources to survive and create something good out of the complexities of life.

Art and Johnnetta renew their vows after five years of marriage.

AN EXQUISITE COMMUNION

Johnnetta B. Cole and Arthur J. Robinson, Jr.
Atlanta, Georgia

As eight-year-old neighbors and schoolmates in 1940s Washington, D.C., Johnnetta Betsch and Art Robinson played, studied and prayed together. Their love, which began in the innocence of childhood, was interrupted for decades, then revived in the public eye.

They were compatible from the beginning. "I liked the fact that she could play all the games—rock school, hide-and-go-seek, Monopoly," says Art. "But what I loved about her was she was just regular. She was my buddy, my friend. She was *cool*."

Their families hailed from Florida, and in Washington they joined the same church. "The neighborhood was full of guys and other young girls, but I was blessed to be able to go to Sunday school with Johnnetta and her sister," Art recalls.

"I remember Art being . . . 'softer' than what often appeared to be very rough and uncaring boys," Johnnetta says. "Art, do you remember when that boy threw a ball and hit the flower pot on Grandma Betsch's porch?"

"Oh, yeah. Richard Robinson [no relation], my best buddy."

"He sure did. And I can't imagine that you would have done that. I also remember you were willing to turn the rope, and I was into some *serious* double dutch. I mean, that was about the best thing a girl could do. It was always hard to get people to turn 'cause everybody wanted to jump. Art Robinson was willing to turn. He was *steady,* always there. I could count on him."

Between the ages of eight and ten, "as much as any young folk could love other young folks, we did that. We loved each other and we were inseparable," Art remembers.

"So at the end of those three years, when my folks said they were moving me and my sister back to Jacksonville, it was really traumatic for Art and me," Johnnetta recalls. "The parting was a serious drama."

"That was the first loss that I had ever experienced in my family—in my *life*," Art says. "I didn't feel any worse when my grandparents died than when Johnnetta and her sister were put in the car and her father drove them away from the front of the house. I fell down on my knees in the street and cried. And I could see that she was on her knees in the back of their car—"

"Bawling!" Johnnetta affirms.

"It was like my world had come to an end," Art says.

For the next five years, when Art's family drove from Washington, D.C., to St. Augustine, Florida, to see his grandmother, he persuaded his parents to stop by Jacksonville to visit Johnnetta. Their last meeting as youths took place when they were fifteen; Art spent a week at Johnnetta's house.

"I was ecstatic!" Art remembers. "Pancakes every morning. She wore a freshly ironed dress, her hair was done and she posed for me on a park bench against a palm tree."

"Doin' my Lana Turner thing." Johnnetta says.

She turned him on to her favorite music—jazz. They browsed through the latest tunes at the record store. "You encouraged me to buy my first record album, *Encore* by Stan Kenton with June Christie, Art Pepper and Maynard Ferguson," Art says. "I'll never forget."

Their lives then took them in different directions, and it was thirty-five years before their paths crossed again. Each had married, had sons and established successful careers—she as a renowned anthropologist, author, professor and administrator at Hunter College and the City University of New York; he as equal employment opportunity officer for the National Library of Medicine at the National Institutes of Health in Bethesda, Maryland, and a real estate and insurance entrepreneur.

On July 1, 1987, Johnnetta made history by becoming the first Black woman to head the nation's leading institution of higher learning for Black women—Spelman College in Atlanta. On July 16, while returning congratulatory phone calls, she came to the phone message slip that said, "Call Art Robinson at the National Library of Medicine." She dialed the number, too preoccupied with working her way through the messages to recognize the name.

"The moment he got on the phone," she says, "I had this *very* strong flash like, 'I know who this is.' When Art came on the line, he asked, 'Do you remember who I am? Do you remember our days in Washington?'

"I said, 'Of course, I do.' Then he said, 'Tell me, do you still like jazz?' Well, that sealed the deal. Because I responded, 'How could you ask me such a question? Don't you remember when I introduced *you* to jazz?'"

They caught up on each other's lives, sharing the news that Johnnetta had been divorced for five years and had three sons, and Art was divorcing and had two sons. They talked about her new job and home. Johnnetta said she liked Atlanta, but missed New York and its live jazz. They made a date to enjoy some of their favorite music at Sweet Basil in Greenwich Village.

A few weeks later, they met in Grand Central Station. "I knew when Art came up the escalator that something very, very special was in process."

Did he feel the same? "I tell you the truth, I had to see how different she looked, because she had a—"

"The girl had *nappy* hair," Johnnetta interrupts, laughing at the contrast to the long, flowing tresses of her youth.

"It was different," he agrees. "But she was so gorgeous. It took me all of five seconds to put her in my arms and hug her."

They went to dinner at Mary Lou's, a restaurant in the Village, and talked until the staff begged them to leave at four the next morning. "I asked if I could see you again," Art says, "and you said, 'Yes.'" Every weekend after that, he flew to wherever she was or they would enjoy a few days in Washington, D.C.

"I had to find a way to get her back," he says. At each visit he gave her one of the pictures he had saved of their early years together. "She just cried."

As Johnnetta mastered the intricacies of running a prestigious college, she and Art enjoyed a "mad, passionate, long-distance courtship." Two months after the reunion, Art proposed on both knees. Because he was in the final stages of his divorce, he and Johnnetta did not get formally engaged until nearly a year later.

Johnnetta worried about Art getting his folks' approval. Her mother and father had passed away years earlier, but she wasn't sure how Art's parents, then eighty-two and eighty-three and still married, felt about his remarriage. Art's folks had no problem blessing the union.

Winning their respective sons' approval was challenging. "I would say it took a lot more time, especially for my oldest, David, who had come to see himself as the central male figure

Drs. Bill and Camille Cosby pose with the newlyweds.

in the family," Johnnetta remembers. "It was not easy. It doesn't happen as an event. People work through things, and I think, for each of our five sons, it's been a process."

They married at Reynolds Cottage, the president's house on the Spelman campus, with a small group of family members and friends, including Drs. Bill and Camille Cosby. Rather than standing with their backs to their loved ones, they switched places with the minister, the Reverend Norman Rates, and faced the gathering.

"Talk about two people being profoundly in love, that's what we were," Johnnetta says. "Nothing was being hidden." They read the poem "Celebration" by Mari Evans to each other as part of the ceremony "because we think the poem was made just for us," Johnnetta confides. "It was the perfect description of two people coming together in their fifties and reinventing the very notion of a love affair."

Celebration

I will bring you a whole person
and you will bring me a whole person
and we will have us twice as much
of love and everything . . .

I be bringing a whole heart
and while it do have nicks and
dents and scars,
that only make me lay it down
more careful like . . .
An you be bringing a whole heart
a little chipped and rusty an
sometimes skip a beat but
still an all you bringing polish too
and look like you intend
to make it shine

And we be bringing, each of us
the music of our selves to wrap
the other in
   Forgiving clarities
  soft as a choir's last
   lingering note our
    personal blend

I will bring you someone whole
and you will bring me someone whole
  and we be twice as strong
   and we be twice as sure
 and we will have us twice as much
  of love
   and everything.

Mari Evans, 1979

They continued their long-distance weekend schedule until Art got a job in Atlanta six months later. Even when they were together full-time, finding the opportunities to enjoy each other wasn't easy. Art balanced a demanding job with educational pursuits and community service. Johnnetta had a nonstop schedule running Spelman, serving on several boards, writing books and speaking around the country.

Their pursuit of private time often took them to romantic getaways. "It could be right around the corner, twenty-five miles down the road or in places like Aruba, Puerto Rico or California," Art says. "We had to turn it off and get into each other."

Johnnetta, who traveled constantly, stresses the importance of being creative enough to find points of communion. "Every morning and every night when I was on the road, we talked. Sometimes it wasn't convenient, but we made sure that we did that because it was a way of touching."

She left romantic notes on his pillow when she went out of town; he still gives her flowers just because she loves them.

They admit that juggling it all has been tough. During hard times, Art says, "I think our relationship just gets stronger, because it's then that I realize how important it is for me to be there for her. She lets me know that she needs me."

At the 1989 Essence *Awards in Atlanta*

While Johnnetta has the higher public profile, she supports Art's dreams as strongly as he does her goals. He had wanted to earn an advanced degree in library sciences and had attended classes on and off over the years, but was too busy with his job and business interests to concentrate on his studies. He confided his desire to Johnnetta; she encouraged him to pursue it. "I was *scared*," he says. "And she would say, 'You can do it. You can do it.' And I listened."

They rarely argue and work to keep differences from becoming annoyances. For instance, Johnnetta says she is "very organized and super-neat," while Art is less so, an issue that came to the forefront at Spelman where they lived and often entertained in the president's house.

They work to overcome conflict with compromise and to keep their very different styles from getting on each other's nerves. They listen carefully, speak openly and take care to respect differing points of view. Both are quick to prescribe a dose of humor as well.

When Johnnetta retired from Spelman in 1997, she took a yearlong sabbatical to enjoy quiet time along with professional pursuits. With the title (for life) of President Emerita of Spelman College, she is now the presidential distinguished professor of anthropology, women's studies and African American studies at Emory University, where she has returned to her first love, teaching.

Though her job title has changed, Johnnetta is still widely recognized and very popular. How does Art keep from feeling threatened and overshadowed by his famous, charismatic spouse? "I know who I am, and I want to be supportive. I want to give my partner as much love as I possibly can," he explains. "And I can't do that if I'm worried about whether the flashbulbs are going off for her and not for me."

Their vision of love is a blend of individual and shared space. Johnnetta sees it as "an image of three circles. There are parts which are really me in ways that are not in intimate connection with Art. And there are ways that are him without being in intimate connection with me. But if you draw a circle that connects those circles, that's where we are and, to me, love is supreme when you don't have to explain that, when there's an understanding that you really are two distinct individuals. If you were the same person, it would be neither as interesting nor as exciting nor, I think, ultimately as moving as when you're different. It's about coming into, on countless occasions, a very exquisite communion."

DWENNIMMEN

RAM'S HORNS

A symbol of strength (in mind, body and soul), humility, wisdom and learning. The strength of a ram depends not so much on the forcefulness of its horns but on the integrity of its heart. It is the learning and wisdom that come with time that enable a person to exceed his or her normal capabilities and excel in his or her endeavors.

Rodgrick and April tie the knot . . .

THICKER THAN BLOOD

April and Rodgrick Coleman
Washington, D.C.

The Coleman house in the picturesque Hillcrest section of southeast Washington, D.C., bustles with the comings and goings of a typical American home. But it's not as conventional as it may seem.

A quartet of youths becomes acquainted as they adjust to the tempo of a stable, loving household. The rhythms of meals, school, church and chores blend with the sounds of television, music, video games and jangling phones.

Presiding over the nonstop activity is a couple barely older than the teens who look to them for guidance, nurturing and love.

At twenty-seven years old, April and Rodgrick Coleman are foster parents to a seventeen-year-old girl and three boys, nine, thirteen and fourteen. "I think we feel a special connection to the older kids because they're the ones that are often left behind," April explains. "Everybody wants the babies, the infants, the toddlers, the elementary-age children. Once they get past that age, there's no one really there for them."

April and Rod marked their fourth wedding anniversary by renewing their vows, adding a passage about their commitment to children—theirs and others'. They took the time to celebrate what they cherish most about each other, from April's focused energy to Rod's sense of humor to their shared passion for improving the lives of young people.

April and Rod didn't set out to become foster parents. When they married in 1993, they talked of adopting a child in the future, and someday maybe having babies of their own. But after working professionally and volunteering with young people, they were driven to do more.

While they were dating, April, who had become a mentor and expert youth advocate, coaxed a reluctant Rod to visit a Washington, D.C., mentoring program that she was involved in. He liked it so much that he became a mentor.

They had neither marriage nor parenting in mind when they entered Howard University in 1989. April Johnson came to the nation's largest public historically Black university from Oakland, California, with plans to become a middle or high school teacher. Rod was fresh out of Long Island, New York, with visions of becoming a college—and eventually, a pro—football player.

They met through mutual friends. "We just kind of meshed," April recalls. "I'm assertive and there are a lot of qualities about him that I needed, like he's really calm and rational." They found it easy to talk with each other about personal matters, goals and dreams. "He was just different. I was able to be very honest with him about some of my insecurities."

April was the one Rod called when, on a visit home from college, his mother told him that her husband—the man Rod had always known as his father—was, in fact, his stepfather, and his real father lived in Texas. April helped him handle the shock and sort out his emotions.

Still, Rod struggled over the conflict between his attraction to April and his feelings for his high school sweetheart back in New York. As a result, he and April drifted apart. April dated others but always believed that she and Rod had a future together.

That belief was tested when Rod's career plans changed. When a string of injuries and illness kept him off the football field, he dropped out of Howard and returned to New York. Then he realized that he had strong feelings for April but didn't know how to express them.

When Rod visited Howard soon after, he and April decided to try again. Back in New York, he started working full-time. He called and visited D.C. whenever he could. "We were building a level of trust because we couldn't physically see each other all the time," Rod says.

After a year and a half of courting long distance, Rod got a job in the D.C. area and moved back to be with April. Soon they became engaged. Some well-meaning folks said that they were too young to marry, advising them to wait until they had their careers together. "I told people, 'I'm content with her; I'm happy with her; this is the one I love and want to share my life with,'" Rod says. "When I've had nothing and all we had was each other to share, she's been there."

April was equally confident in their decision. She appreciated Rod's willingness to relocate, leaving behind the comforts of home to start a new life with her. When he was working and she was a penniless student, he bought her schoolbooks. And she was impressed by the time Rod spent with her nine-year-old brother, Mahir, on his summer visits to D.C. "I knew that somebody who wasn't trying to make a long-term commitment probably wouldn't go through those type of motions."

They credit church-based premarital counseling for opening their eyes to the responsibilities ahead. "Before the counseling I kind of knew what love was," Rod says. "I began to understand that love is not a feeling, it's an action; it's deliberately saying no to myself and yes to her. And her doing the same thing. And receiving; that's how we grow as one. It was impressed upon us that our focal point had to be on God for that oneness to come."

April says that she didn't really think about marriage as a commitment before God until the counseling. "It helped us to define what we really thought love was. They talked about the Bible verse, First Corinthians, Chapter Thirteen, about being patient and bearing all things. I thought, 'Wow, am I gonna be able to bear everything that comes against me? Am I willing to do this?' The counseling helped me to get through that."

They were wed in the middle of April's senior year, on January 1, 1993, at Living Word Ministries Community Church in Oakland, California. In a blend of tradition and personal expression, the bride and groom created the ceremony, writing each word for the minister and themselves, with Mahir serving as Rod's best man. Later, they held a New York reception for East Coast family and friends.

They began married life with rising careers as youth mentors and advocates. Both gained expertise working in several youth-serving agencies.

April, who began tutoring and counseling kids in college, became frustrated when the children she worked with left the program or moved away. As a leader in the Children's Defense Fund Black Student Leadership Network, she helped establish and run Freedom Schools in the Washington, D.C., area.

Rod's volunteer work grew into positions with D.C.'s then-Mayor Sharon Pratt Kelly's Turning Points Program and a Children's Defense Fund Freedom School. Like April, he felt he had found his mission but believed that even a full-time professional contribution wasn't enough. They loved the challenges and satisfaction of helping young people empower themselves. But the problems the kids faced at home seemed insurmountable at times. "It was frustrating because you were with them all day, making all this progress, and then the next day you had to start all over," April said. Rod "wished I could have a kid who could be with me full-time, so that what I teach and what he sees are the same thing."

. . . and reflect upon the wonder of the day

April and Rod started taking kids home for the night or on weekend trips. Their experience with a boy named William made them want to give at least one child a positive, round-the-clock family experience. They applied to become foster parents. While they knew it wouldn't be easy, they say their decision grew from their desire to help some young people by providing a positive, loving home.

A new dimension was added to their lives when, in 1995, Rod "got the call" to serve in the ministry. After volunteering as the director of the Youth Ministry at Metropolitan Wesley AME Zion Church, where he led the youth group in their weekly Bible study meetings and took them on field trips, Rod felt compelled "to study and spread God's word. I just really felt that the Lord wanted me to concentrate my attention upon the young people." He quit his position at the Freedom School to study full-time at Washington Bible College. April continued working while Rod was "in school and in church twenty-four/seven," she recalls. And though money was tight, they managed.

In October 1996, after a seemingly endless eighteen months of training, preparation and waiting to become foster parents, the Coleman household grew from two to six overnight. It took—and continues to take—a great deal of adjustment on everyone's part. The children, April says, "are dealing with issues of separation." All have problems trusting adults. Some have left their natural families; others are devastated after living for years with families they believed would adopt them, only to be put back into the system. Each child attends a different school. In their first year as foster parents, the Colemans saw two of their children adopted and two new children join the family.

"A lot of people didn't think that we would be able to be foster parents because we're so young," April says, "but I think that our age puts us at an advantage because we can relate to the kids and they can relate to us."

After nearly three years of parenthood, Rod and April have had their nerves, their patience and their faith tested many times. Even with all of their experience and training, they admit the challenges are enormous. Working within their boundaries as foster parents—they can't force their beliefs or lifestyle on the children—April and Rod work hard to give them the love, consistency and guidance they may never have had before.

They deal with public challenges to their status as a family. "Sometimes when the older kids call us Mom and Dad in public, people will look and say, 'She's not old enough to be your mother. She must be your play mother,' " April says. "We introduce all of them as our daughters and our sons. Even though we did not birth them, we look at them as ours. These are the kids God has given us to be responsible for."

Part of that responsibility is learning to discipline children who may equal—or exceed—them in size, and handling the inevitable charges of, "I don't have to do what you say. You're not my mother or father!"

"We tell them that, biologically, we're not their parents and we know that," April explains. "We never force them to call us Mom and Dad; we tell them it's their choice."

Physical punishment is not allowed. "It makes you take a look at other forms of discipline," April says. "It forces us to figure out what's behind the child's comment or action. It isn't always easy and I'm not always this rational being," she admits. "There are times when you're thinking, 'This kid needs a spanking.' They know what you can and can't do and they'll test the limits."

Rod and April's faith helps them cope. "We discovered that changing the kids' behavior is no longer our goal," Rod explains, "because you can change that for a moment, get them to do what you want, but unless you change their mind-set, they'll do things that aren't healthy for them when you're not around. Now we're doing a lot of praying and more talking, trying to get to, 'What is it that made you feel so angry and upset that you had to do that?' This lets them talk about their feelings and gives us a platform to talk about how God loves us and how we're supposed to love one another. The kids become more reflective of their behavior, and so it helps."

With every aspect of their lives focused on helping troubled children, April and Rod sometimes feel overwhelmed. When it feels like too much to take, they find ways to give each other time to relax. When things get tense, Rod is apt to crack a joke. "Laughter helps you through the rough times," he says.

"I don't know if I could keep doing it without Rod," April says. "Sometimes when I can't think and I can't take that step back from myself, he's my conscience. He tells me to step back, take a minute and he'll deal with it so I can just go. Likewise, I do that for him. That keeps us going."

Their families offer nonstop encouragement, including reminders that Rod and April pulled some of the same tricks when they were teens. "I thank God because both of our families are very, very supportive of us," April says. "It would be difficult if they weren't."

The foster care organization stays on the case with close contact and ongoing assistance, including a foster parents' support group. That and their religious faith help April and Rod stay focused.

"I think that each one of the children represents something about us that in our relationship we need to change," Rod muses. "For instance, one of the daughters is very concerned about her image around people and I think that's an issue that April and I personally have to deal with—how we're viewed among people. I think that's a task, trying to be who you are and not be defined by others."

Rod struggled with this expectation issue when he started seminary and April worked to support them both. "That was a real change for me because I felt like I was supposed to be working and here she was bearing the weight, and we couldn't pay the bills. But I found that it's not necessarily who's making the income. It's that both people are supporting each other and working towards a goal . . . it's about moving away from what society says 'should be.' "

April balks at well-meaning church members' suggestions that she must look and act a certain way to be a minister's wife; that she should wear skirts and dresses instead of pants, pretend to be less assertive than she is, and keep her opinions to herself. "I don't feel like I fit into that traditional mold. I just process what people say and figure out a way to maintain my individuality."

The Colemans are happy with their lives right now. April works full-time, counseling homeless and runaway youth as service manager at the Washington, D.C., branch of Covenant House, a national agency. Rod left the seminary to more fully devote himself to the home front, and is what the foster care agency calls a family care manager. He facilitates all of their children's educational, medical and legal needs, and advocates for them. He also volunteers with the religious programs for youth at Covenant House.

Rod says he is reaching his goal of working with God's word. "The heart of God is looking after those who can't look after themselves and giving them the love of God," he says. "To look after orphans who cannot do for themselves. That's how I'm able to see what I do in the house as part of my ministry."

He and April find encouragement in the children's progress. "There are days when things are better than good, when they say things they never would have said before, like 'I love you,'" April says. They cite other examples, such as the time one of their daughters used her own money to replace one of Rod and April's favorite compact discs after their collection was stolen. Or when another daughter bought April a T-shirt as an apology after an argument. Or seeing children whose backgrounds made it hard for them to give of themselves becoming excited about presenting April, Rod and one another with Christmas gifts. Rod says he feels rewarded by family moments such as those in which he teaches the kids to help prepare a meal, or they all share a heartfelt hug.

While April and Rod say they would like to adopt children someday, they feel their calling is to serve as foster parents and youth advocates, incorporating their religious faith into everything they do.

"This is God's purpose for our lives," Rod says. "All we're doing is yielding to this purpose. We rely on Him daily; we don't bring glory to ourselves or say the kids are doing better because we've learned this or done that. The résumé means nothing when you've got a kid with tears streaming down his or her face, or they're angry and you have to get to the heart of the problem. You really need God's wisdom and God's love to reach in deep."

Meanwhile, like all parents, April and Rod struggle to make time for togetherness. "How do I give attention to the children and still have enough for my wife, and how does she do the same?" Rod asks. "We've been working it out, just finding our times of the day."

They have discovered the best way to disagree. Rod doesn't like to argue, is quick to jump on the defensive and wants to make up right away. April needs time to express and explore her feelings. Rod is more comfortable with public displays of affection than his wife is. She loves to have friends of their foster kids over for impromptu meals and parties; Rod sometimes prefers peace and quiet.

The hardest part of marriage, April says, is that "you don't think it's going to take so much work." What gets them through is a view of themselves as partners, working together for children—"our covenant relationship, that we are one in our covenant before God. We made a vow before family and God, and that is based on our relationship with Jesus Christ," April says.

She and Rod share a vision of someday opening an organization for young people, "a place of refuge where kids can come and get their needs met," April explains. "That's the type of impact we want to have on children, to change their environment and their hearts," Rod says. "It has grown into a passion."

This couple, young in years but mature in wisdom, understands the power and the necessity of selfless giving.

"Right now our marriage is in the state of focusing on the Lord, because you have to die to your own self in order for you to have life in your marriage," Rod says.

In a tender exchange, they share their appreciation for each other. "When she goes away, even for a day, I feel a loss," Rod says. "When she comes home, there's automatically a smile on my face. When she's around, it's kind of like being filled."

"When I think of Rod, I think about joy because he's always making me laugh, always finding ways to get me to look at the better side of things," April says.

They take the long view of their bond. "Our love is endless, continuous, something that is timeless," says Rod. "Different things can come against it, but true love stands against all of those circumstances."

And holds a very special family together with a force that is thicker than blood.

AKOKO NAN

HEN'S FEET

A symbol of protectiveness and parental discipline tempered with patience, mercy and fondness. A hen may have many chicks and will dig and scratch in the earth to feed them. When parents in Akan society discipline their children, they do so out of love and affection for them. Such parental discipline shows their understanding of life and the protectiveness they offer their children.

April 13, 1968, newlyweds Rachel and Freddie in their first apartment

HOLDING FAST TO DREAMS

Rachel and Freddie Cook
Columbia, Maryland

As she stretched a dime into a dollar for the umpteenth time, Rachel Cook prayed that her husband, Freddie, would find success in his latest business venture. She fought back memories of the comfortable house, fashionable neighborhood and luxury car they had left behind to pursue his entrepreneurial dreams. She swallowed the fear of mounting bills and dwindling cash reserves, fervently hoping that his restless ambition would soon be satisfied.

For thirty-two years, Rachel has believed in and actively supported her man's quest to be his own boss, to be successful and to help other people. She recognizes his vision and knows he is too strong-willed and independent to work for anyone else for long. The ebb and flow of their fortunes have given special meaning to their wedding vow "for richer, for poorer; for better or for worse . . ."

Part of Freddie Cook's drive was growing up "po' " in Atlanta's West End. "We looked up to poor people," he explains. "Poor people don't have the luxuries but at least they could eat. Po' means you don't have enough to eat."

Reared among seemingly indestructible rats and roaches, Freddie and his friends shot birds from the sky for dinner. His parents divorced when he was five, and his mother worked as a maid and a textile inspector to support her three sons.

If poverty made Freddie bitter—"I couldn't understand why I was born to this"—it also fueled his ambition to do well. His first goal was to attend Morehouse College, the historically Black men's college near his house. Watching the proud, studious young brothers stride confidently across campus where Martin Luther King, Jr., had studied, Freddie says he "knew that this school was for me."

Locked into an intense competition with his older brother, Frank, Freddie excelled academically, and at the end of his junior year in high school he was accepted into Morehouse through an early admissions program for outstanding students.

In 1966—his junior year at Morehouse—Freddie met Rachel Strickland, a gorgeous junior at Spelman College, the historically Black women's college across the street. Rachel had ditched two interested suitors so she would be free to meet someone new at the introductory dance on the Morehouse campus.

Freddie not only asked her to dance, but on the second dance told her they would be married and raise kids together. She wrote it off as a line.

She was, he says, "a beautiful Black American princess" with a sheltered upbringing in a comfortable, middle-class southwest Atlanta family. "I always had a vision of the kind of person I wanted to marry—someone sweet, sincere and loving. I had a very unstable childhood and I wanted stability. I looked at her and listened to her and just felt that she was it."

The attraction was mutual. "He was really different from anybody I had ever met. He was very articulate, he could speak on any subject, knew something about anything and everything and seemed to know a lot of people."

She found him demanding, even overbearing, but liked his strength and confidence. He was very protective of her, and she liked that, too. He thought her "tremendously naive," but with his background, he found that refreshing.

They dated all that year. Outside of school, Freddie worked as one of Atlanta's first Black bus drivers. One June evening Freddie whipped out a ring and proposed. He expected Rachel to make him beg, but she surprised him and accepted immediately.

They had heard that it was against the rules for Spelman students to marry, and planned their wedding for the end of their senior year. Two months after their engagement, however,

Freddie grew impatient. After watching his brother get married, he told Rachel that he didn't want a traditional wedding and he didn't want to wait.

Rachel protested that she didn't think she could run a household while keeping up with her studies. Freddie promised to help. The Reverend Dr. Samuel Williams, Freddie's philosophy professor, agreed to perform the service. On Sunday, October 1, 1967, Rachel and Freddie told their parents they were going to church, and with two friends from across town as witnesses, they were wed in the pastor's study at Friendship Baptist Church, which was temporarily housed in the new student union building at Morris Brown College.

A few hours after the nuptials, Freddie changed into his uniform and went back to driving the bus. Rachel returned home, hiding her ring in her purse. They vowed to keep their marriage secret for a year. But, Rachel says, "it was hard to stay apart." Within two weeks, they had an apartment, new furniture and a car.

When Rachel and Freddie told her parents the news, they laughed, thinking it was a joke. After Rachel showed them the apartment and furniture receipts, the laughter turned to silence and, eventually, acceptance.

Though the newlyweds had an apartment, they continued to live with their parents, hiding their rings and their marital status when at school. Then Rachel learned that Spelman students could write to a dean for permission to marry. Reverend Williams helped them with the paperwork, which was approved. In November, Rachel and Freddie moved into the apartment, their marriage no longer secret.

They expected to do well. Freddie, armed with an economics degree, said he planned to get into corporate life, learn the ropes, then go into business for himself. Rachel would teach until the children were born.

Freddie landed a job with Bristol-Myers in Atlanta. Shortly after graduation, he was drafted into the military with plans to go to Vietnam and return "a hero." He left his job and was headed for Officer Candidate School (OCS) when a preinduction physical revealed a cyst on his spine. He was told to have it removed, then come back. You have to take me now, he told them. I've already quit my job. They turned him down and, with his former position already filled, he instantly went "from an OCS candidate to a guy with no job." He painted houses for the next three months.

Then Bristol-Myers offered Freddie another job selling pharmaceuticals in Washington, D.C. He and Rachel moved to a Maryland suburb and Rachel applied for teaching jobs. When she realized she was pregnant, she stopped looking. "I always wanted to be home and raise and teach my children," as her mother had done. Rachel volunteered at a home for unwed mothers until their daughter, Gretchen, was born in 1969.

Freddie was fulfilling the promise of his Morehouse degree. He moved to a company that promoted him to a hospital representative, "a very prestigious position for a Black guy back

June 4, 1968, Freddie graduates from Morehouse.

June 3, 1968, Rachel graduates from Spelman.

then," he recalls. Then he joined another pharmaceutical company and was transferred back home. He and Rachel bought a house in fashionable southwest Atlanta, and topped it off with a Mercedes coupe. "I had a lot of security," Freddie says, "but the whole time I was itching to get out and do my own thing."

Even with a second child, Frederick, born in 1971, Freddie was determined to venture out on his own. He bought a franchise that tinted window glass for businesses in Landover, Maryland, commuting back to Atlanta to see his family.

November 1972, Freddie and Rachel with Gretchen and Frederick

Alone with two small children, Rachel says she was "scared to death." She kept her doubts to herself and maintained the home front. "I feel that you have to make your own way. You pray, but you don't sit and wait on that; you're constantly doing things to make it work." She took in sewing to keep food on the table, working after the children went to sleep, and built a loyal clientele. For a while, Freddie's business was on the upswing, but slow-to-pay government clients eventually forced it to close.

Back in Atlanta, Freddie landed another good sales job. He traveled frequently, but the income was steady. After a few years, he went into business selling cordless telephones, "about twenty-five years ahead of our time," he recalls wistfully.

"By then, Rachel was beginning to have her doubts about me," he says.

"I said, 'Why are you going to do this again?'" Rachel remembers. "'You take a big chance when you go off on your own.' Still, he wanted so much for it to work and I believed in him so much that I said, 'Okay, let's try this again.'"

When little Frederick turned four, Rachel went to work at a child-care center. Her husband, disappointed that things were not going as they had hoped, cried when he dropped his wife off that first day.

Tears or no, Rachel knew they needed the steady, if modest, income from her job.

"During a lot of those times I felt like all we had was each other," Rachel says. "Because a lot of your friends or people who you thought were your friends aren't around anymore."

Although Rachel was concerned, Freddie told her, "Don't worry unless you see me worry." Despite his assurances, she felt his concern, Rachel admits with a tender smile. "There are things that Freddie does when he's worried but he doesn't know that I know. He always had to have the strong face for me."

When Rachel became depressed about things being tough and money being tight, "Freddie would always see the light that I didn't see. He'd say, 'Things are going to be different in a few more weeks.' I believed in him so much that my fears were quickly abated."

The failure of the portable phone venture caused Freddie to doubt himself for the first time. "I felt that I would end up like my father—all promise and no realization. I couldn't take that." He made a few more stabs at the corporate life, and finally found a job that gave him some of the freedom he craved. "I was in a very creative position where I was able to create a product and decide on price. I had not been in that position in a corporate setting before." He stifled the itch for complete autonomy for eight years until, in 1993, he left the company to become an independent contractor and a manufacturer's rep, designing or redesigning packaging and, occasionally, products for companies in the United States and Canada.

At last he feels he has found his niche. Business is up and down, he says. "Things still get rocky sometimes. I am still in the process of becoming successful." He continues to dream of bigger, better ventures, fueled by the longing to help the less fortunate and give Rachel the lifestyle he feels she deserves.

Freddie is quick to credit Rachel's inspiration and support for enabling him to take risks and satisfy his professional yearnings. "There's no way I could have done anything without her being as she is." Her love, support and energy have recharged his spirit throughout the years. "I've always said I didn't deserve Rachel because of her goodness," Freddie confesses. "But I still wanted her."

His desire is matched by Rachel's conviction that, even through the financial ups and downs, Freddie Cook is the right man for her. "I could have walked out of this at any time," Rachel says firmly, her soft voice providing a musical counterpoint to Freddie's booming pronouncements. "He's the person I want and love." With Freddie, Rachel had the one thing she wanted most—"a very stable home and life for my children. My children grew up happy and healthy, knowing they were loved. They had both parents together. To me that means a lot. I always had it and I wanted my children to have it. So I did whatever it took on my part to keep that together. If that meant I had to give up something, I did."

In parenting, as in business, Rachel and Freddie have known both joy and pain. In 1979, their third child, Rodrick, died shortly after birth. The loss hit the family hard, but the birth of Rachel Elon five years later helped them carry on.

Wanting to earn a steady wage while staying home with Elon, Rachel became a licensed home child-care operator. Through good times and bad, she maintained a sense of equilibrium at home. "I always managed to have a balanced meal, but when things were going well, we had a better grade of meat."

Even the cheapest cuts were a step up from the birds Freddie had slaughtered for his boyhood meals. "I came from nothing, so everything we had was a net plus. Our losses were still net pluses for me."

Rachel says the tough times "made us stronger because we knew we had to depend on each other so much to make not only our personal lives successful, but the different businesses and different jobs." She's proud of the fact that "Freddie always knew he had a stable home and a faithful wife who would always be there for him. He loved and adored the children and always enjoyed coming home and being with them."

Though Rachel wouldn't have minded a more financially predictable life, her confidence in Freddie never wavers. "I still love him very deeply," she says softly. "I still hope that his dream is going to be fulfilled." One reason, she explains, is that Freddie's motives are unselfish. He yearns to make it big not for personal gain, but so that he can give to others in need and help young people from backgrounds like his benefit from a chance at higher education.

Rachel recognizes that many women may not have her brand of patience and faith. "I know I have compromised a lot," she says matter-of-factly. "I would not recommend this for everybody. There are no perfect people or perfect situations. You have to decide what you can accept and work with. I did whatever I could to keep my family together."

She knows she could have found a more predictable husband. But that might have bored her, and she wouldn't have grown in the same ways. "I was not a very decisive person. I grew up the youngest child and, in those days, your parents pretty much told you what to do. Knowing how easily a Black person could be hurt living in the segregated South, my parents were very protective and I didn't really have the opportunities to make a lot of decisions. Then, with Freddie working out of town when the children were small, I had to learn to make decisions on my own. I wanted the best for our children and, as a Black mother, I had to fight to make sure they had equal access to everything and were treated fairly in school. I didn't have Freddie there to help me go to battle in those schools."

Freddie's foray into the corporate world increased Rachel's confidence in other ways. "When Freddie started working with these companies, he would be the only Black salesperson. He did very well, so we would be invited to a lot of dinners and evening affairs. I was rather quiet, and I had to learn to talk to all these different people. Since they didn't know us or many of our people, I felt I had to prove that we were human, so I always talked about our family's best qualities, to let them know that we do things like everybody else. In the beginning it was scary because I wasn't used to being around Whites. Then I saw that I could socialize with people of any race with no real problems."

Through the years of changing fortune, Rachel has steadfastly pursued a dream of her own. After working for several years as a teacher, education administrator and curriculum specialist, the former French major is pursuing her college goals. She is now a "full-time student with a part-time job," earning a master's in instructional systems development with a concentration in early childhood education at the University of Maryland/Baltimore County while working as a graduate assistant. She had hosted several international students, including four from France, in an international exchange program, all of whom have invited her to visit their homes. When the time is right, Rachel says, she will take them up on their offers.

For now, she is content to serve as her family's anchor and her husband's biggest fan. Comparing herself to the tortoise and Freddie to the hare, Rachel says, "I guess we've created a pretty good balance. I'm stable, consistent and grounded, and he has brought a lot of excitement to my life. I always liked that part of Freddie that was wild, crazy and risky. It was thrilling because I was so conservative and down-to-earth. He has definitely spiced up my life."

There's been plenty of sugar, too. After more than three decades of marriage, Rachel and Freddie are openly affectionate, trading "lots of hugs, kisses, pats and tickles," Rachel says, along with words of devotion. One Christmas, Freddie presented Rachel with a plaque bearing a poem he had written her in college. In a note addressed to *"Mi vida, mi esposa futura"* (To my life, my future wife), he wrote:

> *And when the lights of heaven dim,*
> *When moments cease to be,*
> *My love, for you, will be there too,*
> *Beyond eternity.*

Both cherish these reminders of the love that helps them balance their differences and find satisfaction in tackling new challenges. With Gretchen recently married, Frederick married with three children, and Rachel Elon in high school, they see a future full of new possibilities. Freddie is not so comfortable with his present circumstances that he has stopped envisioning the Next Big Thing. He tells the tennis team he coaches that "winning is a state of mind. When you're behind in points, you're not necessarily behind. In order to be a winner, you have to see success up ahead. And I see it. If you don't, you're a loser. You've got to have the dream to keep going."

OSRAM

THE MOON

A symbol of faith, patience, understanding and determination. As a proverb says, "It takes the moon some time to go 'round the nation." Osram also means faith, the belief in oneself and the things that are meaningful, faith that helps one soar above the pettiness of a situation or the narrowness of some situations in life. Patience is the practical expression of faith, hope, wisdom and love.

Joycelyn and Oliver after her confirmation as U.S. surgeon general in September 1993

AFTER THE GAME

Joycelyn and Oliver Elders, Jr.
Little Rock, Arkansas

Washington, D.C.—December 8, 1994. President Bill Clinton had asked her to resign as U.S. surgeon general for suggesting masturbation as a safer-sex alternative for young people. The media were not only going to town on the controversy, but reporting that her son, Kevin, had been arrested on drug-related charges. Pondering her next move, Dr. M. Joycelyn Elders said her prayers and went to sleep.

She awakened to find her husband, Oliver, sitting up in bed saying, "Sug, let's go home."

Home . . . to Arkansas, the land that had nurtured, shaped and loved them. Where Joycelyn, born Minnie Jones, had grown up chopping cotton in Schaal near Nashville, Arkansas, and worked as a maid to get through college, rising to director of Arkansas's Health Department. Where Oliver, who hailed from De Witt, had been a quarterback and captain of his high school's state champion basketball team, a point guard on his college basketball team, a pro player with the Harlem Magicians and the winningest high school basketball coach in Arkansas history, and was every bit as renowned as his high-profile wife.

The controversy that engulfed them in Washington, D.C., didn't faze the Elders. Before a 1993 presidential appointment as U.S. surgeon general was even a possibility, Joycelyn and

Oliver Elders had weathered some serious storms. From the loss of Joycelyn's beloved brother and sister, Oliver's debilitating depression and the stillbirth of their third child, to nursing Oliver's mother through Alzheimer's disease, taking in a sick White foster child and facing the painful truths of their son Kevin's drug and alcohol addition, the doctor and the coach found comfort in each other.

"Usually when we're in trouble, that's the time when we have been most supportive," Joycelyn says. "That's the time when we can come together and really try to talk. One thing that I know is that, in troubled times, Oliver has always been there. I know I walk around feeling that there's just not a crisis out there that's so big that the two of us can't handle it. And if we can't handle it and fix it, then it can't be fixed."

When asked to resign as surgeon general for suggesting teenagers be taught that masturbation is an acceptable substitute for riskier sexual behaviors, Joycelyn learned that the honest intelligence, straight talk and commitment to real-world solutions that had served her well in Arkansas were not valued in Washington, D.C.

On December 1, 1994, Joycelyn spoke at the World AIDS Day Conference at the United Nations. At a panel discussion following her speech, a psychiatrist asked about discussing and promoting masturbation as a way to curb the spread of HIV. "I might have squirmed a little at that, but not much," she writes in her autobiography, *Joycelyn Elders, M.D.* "I told him I was a strong advocate of comprehensive health education that was age-appropriate and complete, and that children had to be taught all the things they needed to know." To clarify her point she added, "In regard to masturbation, I think that is part of human sexuality, and perhaps it should be taught."

No one, including the roomful of media people at the conference, reacted to her remark, and it received no news coverage.

Several days later, U.S. Secretary of Health and Human Services Donna Shalala called Joycelyn into her office to ask whether she had mentioned masturbation at the U.N. AIDS conference. Joycelyn answered that she probably had. Secretary Shalala asked whether she had said that masturbation ought to be taught in schools. Unable to remember exactly what she said, Joycelyn said she believed that had been the case.

Secretary Shalala said that was "too much" and that she would have to discuss it with White House Chief of Staff Leon Panetta. Moments after Joycelyn returned to her office, Mr. Panetta called to ask for her resignation.

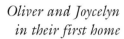

Oliver and Joycelyn in their first home

Joycelyn said she wasn't leaving "unless my president asks me to."

"Despite Panetta, I still wasn't thinking about resigning," she writes. "I expected that Clinton and I would probably sit down and have a conversation. Of course, the far right had been demanding my resignation practically every time they got on the air. But Clinton and I had stood side by side in some pretty rough fights" in her six years as director of the Arkansas Health Department. Soon, President Clinton did call and apologize before asking Joycelyn to resign.

She considered her options. Despite the president's request, no one could force her to resign the four-year appointment, though she would have been, as she says, "a surgeon general with no staff, nothing." She could have stayed in the U.S. Commission Corps or taken another, less visible position in the Clinton administration. After all, the nation's capital was exciting and Oliver enjoyed his job with the U.S. Department of Education.

But once he uttered the words, "Sug, let's go home," the solution seemed crystal clear.

Joycelyn and Oliver relaxing in their Little Rock home after her resignation

They had their home in Little Rock, as well as several rental properties. They wanted to be near Kevin and close to the land where their love had taken root and blossomed.

"I was really going through turmoil," Joycelyn says. Kevin had been incarcerated on what may have been a trumped-up drug charge—some believed that he was set up by police—and "it was a very painful, difficult time for us. We talked to each other a lot about Kevin and what we could and could not have done," Joycelyn shares.

"We could have stayed in Washington, D.C.," Oliver muses. "But with her losing her job, that was not a place for us to be."

Joycelyn's knack for causing a stir got Oliver's attention when they met in 1959. As a fourth-year medical student at the University of Arkansas Medical School, Joycelyn was sent to Horace Mann, Little Rock's only Black high school, to administer the school basketball team's required annual physical exams. Coach Oliver Elders, in a hurry to begin practice, had the boys strip down to their shorts before the doctor arrived.

When she walked in, stunning in a navy blue suit, Oliver thought she looked out of place and directed her to the upstairs offices. "You asked for a doctor, didn't you?" she replied. "If you want these guys examined, I'm the doctor."

Oliver's mouth fell open. He'd never even heard of a woman doctor. Neither had the boys, who began running around, shouting "Oh, ain't nobody gonna be lookin' at me." Oliver calmed them down by offering to get his exam (which wasn't required) first. Reluctantly, the boys followed, and emerged mellowed by Joycelyn's warm manner and cool professional charm.

Oliver, who had checked out the alluring young doctor from the very beginning, offered Joycelyn the season basketball pass that had always been the school's thank-you gift to the examining physician.

"It's a fact that I was interested," she writes in her autobiography. "I had noticed Oliver the first moment I walked into that gym. As tall and handsome as he was, it would have been hard not to."

He says he handed her the pass; she says he forgot, then called her to say he'd bring it to her. In any case, she went to the games, pleased when he'd look for her in the stands, and they'd acknowledge each other with a nod. While she didn't know much about basketball, spending time with the coach made her a student—and serious fan—of the sport.

They saw each other a lot—"as friends," Joycelyn says. "He'd always take me to the games, but he was telling me about his girlfriend."

After the games, the two would "talk all night" about their lives, dreams and goals.

Both had been married before and divorced. Both were devoted to their careers and fiercely committed to being the very best. "One of the things that separates success from failure is dedicating yourself to it," Oliver says. "And to the person who seems to be in step with you. You've both got to want to be successful. You've both got to want to make the sacrifices for it. When we talked and identified what was important, we were talking about the same things."

As Joycelyn prepared to go to the University of Minnesota for an internship interview, Oliver said he had to take his girlfriend to a dance over in Memphis. When he changed those plans to drive Joycelyn north for her interview, she "knew then that I didn't have to worry too much about this girlfriend."

By the time they returned from Minnesota a few days later, Joycelyn and Oliver were in love and committed to each other. They married two months later, on Valentine's Day 1960.

While longer courtships may be necessary for some, Oliver says, "Things seem to have fallen into place for us. There's a magnetism about people, how you feel when you're in their presence, how the things you do and the things they do seem to suggest that you are compatible. The things that you talk about are more or less in sync. The things you seem to want are in sync.

"You get a comfortable feeling. It's almost like putting on a three-piece suit that fits. You check it out, you try it on, you get the feel, and then you look in the mirror and you like everything that you see. If I had to do it over again, I would do it exactly the same way because it fit then and it fits now."

The newlyweds moved into the room Oliver rented near Horace Mann high. Months later, Joycelyn accepted a yearlong internship at the University of Minnesota. Before marrying Oliver, she had planned to complete her internship, pediatric residency and surgical residency there. When her internship ended, however, rather than have Oliver leave his career, she went back to Arkansas to become a pediatric resident.

While Oliver spent the summer at a graduate program in health and physical education at Indiana University, Joycelyn found a small house in North Little Rock and began her residency at University Hospital, where she taught, doctored, conducted pediatric rounds and supervised medical students and interns. Residents worked all day, that night and the next day, then went home to be on call.

When Oliver returned from Indiana, his nighttime visits to the hospital to keep her company during her breaks or simply lend moral support when she was too busy to talk helped Joycelyn endure the brutal schedule.

Oliver was her rock during the hardest times, such as the night when several young patients died, or when she had to treat sexually abused children. The most horrific case was a six-month-old girl who had been raped by a teenage baby-sitter and left torn and bleeding. Though surgery saved the baby's life, Joycelyn needed an outlet for the horror and grief that filled her. "You bury sights like that somewhere inside of you," she writes. "But if that's all you do with them, you will eventually find yourself in serious trouble. I'm not sure where my colleagues got their solace. I got mine from knowing that Oliver was there."

In Joycelyn's second year of residency, their son Eric was born. When her maternity leave ended, extended family helped care for the baby. At a few weeks old, Eric was attending his father's basketball games. The busy Elders family thrived.

In 1963, Joycelyn became chief pediatric resident at the hospital, an honor under any circumstances and unheard of for a Black female in Arkansas. The work was demanding, and she had to overcome the deeply ingrained racism of some of her staff and parents of her patients. "As chief, I would be head of nine other residents, all of them White southern males . . ." she writes, "and no one would be used to working on an even basis with someone like me. I'd also have to deal with doctors all over the state, and in some parts of Arkansas old-time attitudes hadn't changed." In a telephone conversation, a referring physician she'd never met in person described the patients he was sending her as "good ol' cotton patch niggers." Still, Joycelyn persevered and excelled. Racism aside, she writes, "When you're successful . . . when you heal somebody's child, parents think you are not just good, you are super good. They think you are better than you are."

Their family life intensified. Joycelyn and Oliver's second son, Kevin, was born in August 1965. They had read about Montessori schools and helped to start one that Eric attended in Little Rock. When they weren't working, Oliver and Joycelyn spent every spare moment with the boys. Life was hectic, but good.

Then, when Kevin was about nine months old, Oliver became depressed, withdrawing into a shell, losing his temper and sitting for hours in a near-catatonic state. Both Oliver and Joycelyn sought psychiatric help, but it got so bad that Joycelyn decided she couldn't take it anymore. When Oliver got better, she decided, she would take the boys and leave. That's when the psychiatrist told her that Oliver would never recover.

But Oliver started taking medication and gradually began to emerge from his shell. One day, Joycelyn, fed up with walking on eggshells and trying to keep the boys quiet, screamed out her pent-up anger to her husband. And, for the first time in a long time, he responded. She learned to express her needs and feelings more openly, and Oliver slowly returned to his old self.

Both Oliver and Joycelyn were renowned in their fields and received numerous job offers both in and outside of Arkansas. Early on, they agreed that they wouldn't move if it would hurt either career. When she was offered the position of surgeon general, Joycelyn told President Clinton that she wouldn't go to Washington, D.C., without Oliver. The president began thinking of a suitable position for the popular coach.

"I've never believed in her living in one place and me in another," Oliver says. "Wouldn't work for me. I think that if you're married, you need to be together. There's too much you need to talk about. You need to be there; that's important." In Little Rock, they not only had job security, but the chance to ride to work and eat lunch together. "What better situation than that?" Oliver asks.

Over the years, the Elderses' happiness has been tempered with a series of heartfelt losses. Joycelyn worked through her third pregnancy in 1967. A few days before her due date, she noticed that the baby wasn't moving. The doctors checked her, induced labor and delivered a baby boy, stillborn with the cord wrapped around his neck. Knowing that the baby would have been severely brain-damaged had he lived, the couple grieved and made peace with their fate.

Joycelyn's brother, Bernard Jones, who she writes was the first Black veterinarian in Arkansas, was murdered in 1978 by a man who had been stalking Bernard and his wife for some time. "There was something unbelievable about losing Bernard. It was so awful to think that someone could live such a completely kind and friendly life yet be struck down the way he was. The jury convicted Bernard's killer and sentenced him to life without parole. The pain this man caused still lies heavy on us all, even though it's been . . . years now. None of us wanted him put to death, but I can't say there's much forgiveness in our hearts either."

In 1986, Joycelyn's younger sister, Pat, died from injuries sustained in a car accident. The Elderses offered to help Pat's husband, Sidney, rear their three children—two girls and a boy—but he managed to keep the family together and become a "Superdad."

A more elusive family member was Nina, an eight-year-old diabetic White girl with alcoholic parents and an unstable home life When Nina, a former patient of Jocelyn, was twelve, things got so bad that she asked to stay with the Elderses for a while. Joycelyn, who had taken in patients and other young folks, said okay. At fifteen, Nina asked if she could live with them permanently. With Eric and Kevin away at college, Joycelyn agreed. She took foster-parenting classes, fought to get Medicaid coverage for Nina and enrolled her in high school. After a while, Nina started running away and finally quit school to party with a man who was much older. Nina's antics were stressful for Joycelyn and Oliver, who were already worried about Kevin. They lost touch with Nina, and they were devastated when, years later, Nina was found murdered.

Being there for each other in challenging times is a theme that runs through their lives and their marriage. In facing personal and professional challenges, Joycelyn and Oliver take it back to supporting each other through triumphs and defeats. "In times of winning, you don't have to support him," Joycelyn says. "Everybody else does. You stand off to the side and everybody else is around him and you can't get there. In times of losing, there's usually nobody there, so when it becomes obvious that he's gonna lose, I don't care where I am in the gym, I start making my way down so that, when it's over, I'm right there."

"The important thing is to have somebody there with me," Oliver says. "After a hard ball game, and one where we're not successful, she would just *be* there. She'd come sit and I'd look over there and our eyes would meet. And she'd say, 'Tough game.' And I'd say, 'Yeah, sure was.' "

Tougher than losing any basketball game was Kevin's drug and alcohol abuse. Their good-natured second son, who had battled a childhood kidney disease, struggled with his weight well into his teens. A stomach stapling operation made the pounds come off but didn't address the underlying problems that had driven him to overeat. In Kevin's second year of college at the University of Arkansas at Fayetteville, he began to drink, returning to Little Rock under the influence. Eventually, he dropped out of school.

His parents weren't certain whether to get Kevin professional treatment or let him handle his addiction on his own. They watched, worried, prayed and discussed their difficulties. "You want so much for your children; you want for them to do well," Oliver says. "They may not be doing well at this point in life. It doesn't mean that down the road they're not going to do well. If you love them and care for them, you're always going to be concerned.

You'll have certain ways that you conduct your affairs with them. And you and your spouse are going to have to come to a meeting of the minds as to how you do that."

Oliver and Joycelyn say that even though their sons are grown, they still sometimes disagree about how to treat them. "The way you handle it is to be as loving as you can and keep communicating, with your children and with each other," she says.

Coming to grips with raising families is very difficult, Oliver says. "Children are little puzzles that we're trying to put together. We don't always agree on how to get them from point A to point B. But the thing we've always done is that we *talk* about it. We mix it up and then we talk about it again, and we try to come to some kind of consensus. When it doesn't come out right, we don't explode and throw our hands up and say, 'That's it!' "

It's not always simple. "Sometimes we have real blowouts, and we strongly disagree," Joycelyn says. "We've learned to just keep arguing till we've got it right."

One thing they never argued about was how to help and care for family members. Early on they agreed that "whatever he decided for his family, that's what we would do and I wouldn't argue about it. He would go along with whatever I decided for my family.

"All during this time when my sisters and brothers were trying to go to college, we had to borrow money sometimes to help them, but he just said, 'Well, Sug, we'll have to see if we can get it.' " Arguing about family, she says, "is a battle you can't win."

So when Oliver's mother developed Alzheimer's disease and needed care, "there wasn't a decision to make," Joycelyn remarks. "The decision was how to get everything done. You just get into it and it evolves." Eric and Kevin pitched in to help, and Oliver's mother moved in with them and received the best of care until her death in 1993.

When the Elderses returned to Little Rock from Washington, D.C., Joycelyn left public service to work as a pediatric endocrinologist at the University of Arkansas. As she writes in her autobiography, "None of the essentials has changed. I'm a physician. I'm Black and female. I've been poor. I've been through it. I'm still here, and I'm still in the fight." She retired in 1999, still speaking and writing about public-health issues, especially those related to children.

Coach Elders, as he is reverently referred to by Arkansans, oversees their rental properties and business interests. While admitting that he sometimes longs for the coaching job that was part of his life for thirty-six years, he says it's "not something that I can't do without. I don't think I need to go back into it because my retirement's good, my business is good and my marriage is intact."

They count their blessings, too, that Kevin seems to be on the road to recovery.

The self-described workaholics admit that they could make more time for romantic dates. They're often so tired that relaxing in their comfortably elegant home is the most pleasurable thing they can imagine.

In a tender moment, the coach turns to the doctor, and in a smooth baritone, serenades her as he did recently at a fraternity gathering, with the Kappa Alpha Psi "Sweetheart Song":

You're as pretty as a picture,
and you're sweet as you can be.
I love you so sincerely;
you're all the world to me.
And if ever I should lose you,
it would really break my heart.
I love; I adore you,
for you're my Kappa Alpha Psi Sweetheart . . .

The former surgeon general, who wears the mantle of power as comfortably as her own skin, gazes raptly as her husband showers her with song. And it's clear that home is exactly where "Sug" wants to be.

ODO NYERA FIE KWAN

LOVE NEVER LOSES ITS WAY HOME

A symbol of devotion, implying the strong bond between married couples or lovers. An Akan proverb states that "a loved one does not get lost on the way to a loved one's home."

Inell and Bruce's wedding

"FOR THE LOVE OF YOU"

Inell and Bruce Ellis
Arlington and Culpepper, Virginia

Ⅰn 1990, Inell Ellis had already left Bruce and moved herself and their three children into her mother's house. She loved her husband and longtime sweetie with all her heart, but couldn't deal with his drug addiction and running the streets anymore.

Bruce would arrange to meet her, away from the disapproving eyes of Inell's parents and the sad faces of Joey, eight, Justin, six, and Kristin, four. He begged Inell to come back, promising that he'd change. She longed to believe him. . . .

Then one day she came home from work to the news that the police had been to the house and wanted Inell to call them. "My heart just dropped," she says. The police asked Inell whether she'd seen Bruce, and told her about the reward money she could collect for helping them find him. "I told them I hadn't seen him," she recalls. "That night, when he came to the house, I asked him what was going on. He said he'd taken part in an armed robbery and was planning to run from the law. Then he asked me what he should do. I said, 'You should turn yourself in because I'd be worried. I wouldn't know if you were dead or alive, and I'd feel a whole lot better if you'd turn yourself in.' "

Bruce surrendered to the police and received a long sentence for taking part in the robbery. Since no shots were fired and no one was hurt, Bruce was told that, with luck, he may get out after serving thirteen years.

He and Inell didn't know when he'd be released or what might happen to him inside, but they figured that prison would at least give him a fighting chance to shake his crack cocaine addiction and ponder the error of his ways.

Having replaced his drug habit with faith in the Lord, Bruce is serving that sentence "one day at a time." While time drags for him in a concrete cell, it races past Inell, who tries to keep one step ahead of the demands of helping run a child-care center and rear three near-teen children on her own. There's never enough energy, money or time, rarely a chance to answer Bruce's frequent letters or gather a thought for herself.

Sometimes she's tempted to give up hope, but then she rewinds her memory for a glimpse of happier times.

It was October 1976 in Arlington, Virginia, where she and Bruce both grew up. Inell Buchanan was sixteen and a junior in high school when she met Bruce Ellis, eighteen, through mutual friends. The first time she saw him, she said, "That's the guy I want." He was outgoing and spontaneous; she was quiet and introverted.

"He looked like he was a lot of fun," she says. Bruce liked the way she looked and started flirting. "There was just something about her; she was IT."

They hung out with a group of friends and became buddies. "I really don't know how we got started talking," Bruce says, "but we'd spend hours on the phone at night. We'd talk, fall asleep, wake back up and talk some more." Bruce loved Inell's gentleness and air of stability, while his spontaneity and sense of humor appealed to her romantic nature. "We'd do fun things out of the blue, like he'd pick me up and we'd go to the fair or sit in the park," she recalls. "And he'd always keep me laughing."

On July 4, 1976, they were sitting on a blanket in the park listening to their favorite song, "For the Love of You" by the Isley Brothers, when they kissed for the first time.

"We really started dating after the kiss," Inell says. Her parents were pretty strict and didn't exactly approve, but they didn't stop Inell from seeing Bruce.

"Bruce wasn't your average 'good' teenager; he had been in detention centers and things like that, so my parents didn't approve of that. But while we were dating, he didn't get into trouble."

They dated on and off while Inell finished high school. Around the time she graduated, Bruce went to prison for armed robbery. He stayed there during the four years that Inell

(From left) Kristin, Bruce, Inell and Justin during a visit

attended college, first at Morgan State University in Baltimore, Maryland, then at North Carolina A&T University in Greensboro.

They wrote to each other regularly, and when Inell came home for the summers, she visited Bruce in prison. While in college, Inell wasn't interested in dating others, she says, because she was still emotionally attached to Bruce. "I honestly didn't see him as a less suitable partner

Eldest son Joey

because he was in jail, because I had been with him prior to that and I knew he was a good person who had made a bad choice.

"I felt like I knew that we would be together when he came out. My mind was set that he was the one for me, so I wasn't really looking for or open to other relationships. I never thought about getting involved with someone and saying I don't want to see Bruce anymore. I thought about getting through school and him getting out and us being together. Because I liked the relationship we had prior to him going in."

Sometimes, Bruce got out on furlough so they could see each other, and they introduced physical intimacy into their relationship. When she graduated at twenty-three with a degree in child development, Inell learned that she had become pregnant from one of those furlough visits.

Bruce, having resolved to change his ways, found a job, then proposed. Inell readily accepted. "We wanted to wait until we had gotten a place and gotten settled in that way," Inell says. Joseph was born in November 1982. The couple was wed in a beautiful outdoor ceremony on July 2, 1983.

The early years of their marriage were nearly ideal. Inell worked as a day-care teacher and Bruce as a building supervisor for the Fairfax County Public Schools. They had Justin in March 1984, then moved to a townhouse in Chantilly, Virginia. Kristin was born in December 1985. Though Inell's pregnancies were difficult and all three babies had been born prematurely, they grew into healthy children.

Inell moved up to director of a day-care center on an Army base and Bruce was promoted to the head of maintenance for the third largest high school in the county. They found a larger townhouse in Manassas, Virginia.

Best of all was abundant family time. "We had a lot of outings and visits with family members," Inell says. "Bruce worked a lot, but when he was home, we'd try to do things together."

"Those were the best years that we had, because we spent all of our time together, did everything together," Bruce says. "I was a happy father, and a happy husband, too."

Then Bruce started running the streets with his single friends. "I think he felt like he could be married, but do 'single' things," Inell says. "I was frustrated a lot, but being the timid person I was at that time, I just let it happen." She swallowed her anger and focused on mothering. "If it wasn't for the kids, I think I would have had a nervous breakdown. I never let them see me cry."

Inell suspected that Bruce was using drugs, but didn't want to believe it. She knew that he was prone to dangerous pastimes because he had spent most of his childhood in foster homes "without a male or father figure."

The pain of childhood abandonment haunted him. When his birth mother put Bruce and his brother in foster care, she never kept her promise to come and take them home. "I can remember my mom was getting ready to leave and I was standing on the porch watching her pull off. And I made up my mind that nobody was gonna hurt me again. I built a wall around my heart," Bruce says.

As an adult, Bruce's frustration and lingering anger led him to a cocaine addiction. His employer held his job and tried to get him in a drug treatment program. But Bruce says he "had too much pride and not enough sense to go."

He began working extra jobs, relying on the cocaine for extra energy. "Then someone introduced me to crack, and I was on my way towards the downfall."

Bruce went to work and began selling crack "on a minor level, to friends. Then it gets to the point where you're your own best customer. I'd say, 'I'm gonna spend a hundred dollars,' and that turned into several hundred, and the next thing you know, the check's gone and you're so frustrated, you just go ahead and do the rest of it. Smoking crack is like chasing a ghost that never comes back. You always try to get the euphoria of that first high again.

"I had this family and . . . there was a war taking place inside of me where I *wanted* to do what was right, but I didn't know how. Sometimes I'd come home at night and sit there and cry. I just didn't know how to get myself back straight.

"When I came home from the pen [the first time], I felt like I had to prove something to Inell's family and to my family. Once I had done well in the county and had mastered my job and had my staff in order and was getting awards, it was like, 'You've done it now.' As long as that challenge was there, it was all right. When that challenge wasn't there, I didn't know what to do. Now that I think about it, I was afraid of success. Even though I wanted it, when I got it, I was afraid of it."

When Inell tried to talk about his problems, Bruce, "not knowing how to deal" with the subject, would leave.

"When things got real bad, I asked her why she didn't hate me. She told me that she hated some of the things I did and the way I was acting, but inside she loved me and believed she always would."

Just before the 1990 armed robbery, Bruce considered fleeing to New York, or committing suicide so that Inell and the children would least have the insurance money.

During their separation before the robbery, he and Inell would meet at the mall and talk "about my life being a wreck." Bruce, who had always liked feeling that he had the answers, couldn't offer any solutions to his dilemma.

He says now that police hunting for him "was God's mercy coming to me. I sensed it was time for me to get locked up. I was beginning to see how what I was doing was affecting so many people."

When he asked Inell what he should do, "I knew I didn't want to leave her; I didn't want just to take off and not be able to come back. That wasn't an option."

Once he was in jail, "it was like déjà vu. I never thought I'd be locked up again. I fell to my knees and cried, 'God, if you're real, do something with my life, 'cause I can't do this anymore.' Something happened on that floor inside my heart, and my life hasn't been the same since. I felt like I had a release on the inside of my heart. I didn't have any bright lights, but I had a knowing on the inside that, somehow, everything was gonna be okay."

Despite his love for Inell, Bruce worried that it wasn't fair to expect her to wait for his release. Because he didn't know how long he might be imprisoned, he told her to forget about him and move on.

She replied that she would stick with him, that they'd hang in there and see what happened, day by day. The first year he was in, she "cried a lot, because it was just difficult. I didn't have a car, wasn't making a whole lot of money and struggled to pay the bills."

Bruce kicked his drug habit and became an ordained minister. "Since he's been in, we've talked about how he didn't trust because of his childhood," Inell says. "I think if he was to come home now, he would know how to be a husband and a father.

"I still love him and I look forward to him coming home, even though the kids are going to be nearly grown then. During the time he was doing drugs, he cheated on me. The marriage to me was pure, and he tainted it. I've forgiven. I just can't forget everything.

"There have been times during the years when I've said I'm going to tell him I can't do this anymore. But I don't want to do that." No matter what, Inell says, she comes back to the belief that she and Bruce are meant to be together forever.

"When people ask, 'Why are you waiting on him?' I say, 'Because he's my husband and I love him.' And he's a good person, you know. Whenever anybody says, 'Go on and divorce him!' . . . I've never thought about that. It isn't something I want to do. I just want to be with him. I can't imagine being with someone else. I don't picture myself being with or marrying anyone else. He's my family."

She struggles to cope; he tries to understand what she's going through, while wrestling with his feelings of guilt and helplessness. Straining to hold the home front together and keep three teens on the straight and narrow, Inell worries that her children will have spent too much of their childhood without their father. She wishes that Bruce were at her side, helping her with the day-to-day, instead of being so near and yet so far.

Her spirits have been lifted by the news that he may be released in 2003. Compared to the years of not knowing how long his sentence may be, "I think that will be more of a breeze. Now that the kids are older, they're easier to deal with. Recently, someone offered to help renovate our house. I told Bruce I'm looking forward to him coming home so we can do things like home improvements together."

Their time apart has made her much stronger, she says, more assertive in talking with her husband, whether questioning his actions or verbally expressing her love. "In the past, I didn't say what I felt, but I do now," something she says that Bruce has always wanted her to do.

Inell realizes that when Bruce does come home, they'll both be very different people from the couple they once were. Along with being drug-free and devoutly religious, "Bruce is more serious now, not as humorous as he was then. He may be challenged by my independence." But she is optimistic that things will work out.

Bruce hopes, too, and prays constantly. He maintains the connection to his family through letters of love and encouragement, pouring out his emotions and expressing his devotion.

Inell devours every word and answers in her heart, but rarely has time to put pen to paper in response. "Sometimes he gets impatient with me about not writing him. I tell him it doesn't mean I don't want to, but there's a lot of things going on out here."

Their telephone conversations are limited to fifteen minutes at a time. "Sometimes when I call, there are things I want to tell her, but I just let her talk and get it all out. My wife and I have learned how to talk since I'm incarcerated this time," Bruce says.

While Inell carries on outside, Bruce adapts to the numbing routines and "hostile atmosphere" of prison. He shares a two-man cell that is "about twelve by eight with a double bunk, a toilet, a bench and two lockers. You get shut in at nine-forty-five at night and come out at six-fifteen in the morning." He says he's blessed to be able to have a television in his cell. He stows his family pictures in an album, but finds it painful to look at them too often.

Through letters, calls and visits, Bruce catches glimpses of his children's emerging personalities. "Joseph is very athletic. Kristin's an active young girl. Justin's a little more laid back," he says.

Faith in God and in his wife keeps Bruce going. "I know Inell. I trust her word. It's evident that I have the best wife in the world. She's a good mother, she's my best friend. I believe God has shown me his love through her, and what love really is. I believe she deserves better. I hurt more for her than I do myself. I have made up my mind and I'm doing everything now to ensure that I'm not the same when I leave as when I came in.

"I've given my heart to the Lord. Since then I've been called to minister and been ordained. I've found out that I'm not such a bad person. And I'm very possibly gonna get out of here and be successful and handle that success better than I did before. And if I do, it's gonna be because of Him."

When the guilt and loneliness wash over him, "It's so good to know that Inell's there, that she's going to be there. I also feel hurt, 'cause I know that she knows I'm not the same person, but I'm sure she still has questions, doubts, maybe fears that this will happen again.

"Thinking of her, I can't help but think of love. You really can't talk about love unless God is involved, because He is love. And when you find true love, you can't help but acknowledge it.

"I believe we have a supreme love that is not based on me being locked up or the wrong that I've done because I know that my wife loves me in spite of that. That's one of the things I've learned through her—that in spite of what people say or do, I really love her and can still want good for her. Our loves goes beyond the touch-feely thing.

"Inell's mother told me that when a relationship starts out with friendship, when love isn't kickin', friendship will last. That's probably why we're still married. We really became friends before we were involved with one another, and that's one of the things that kept us going."

It's the sweet sounds of the Isleys that keeps their spirits linked: their favorite album, *Three Times Three,* with *their* song, "For the Love of You," which he plays to transport him beyond his tiny cell and she hums beneath her breath to recall the loving warmth of his embrace.

Each endures the present by creating a vision of the future. Inell imagines rocking with Bruce on the porch, enjoying sunrises and sunsets side by side. He envisions them slow dancing, to the song they first kissed to, the sound track of their growing love. And for a moment, their heartbeats synchronize, united in a vision that is equal parts memory and hope.

HYE-WO-NHYE

UNBURNABLE

A symbol of toughness, imperishability and permanency of self or a leader. To survive in the world, a person must be able to endure hardships. Though adverse situations may affect someone, he or she still manages to endure, stand tall and come out ahead. Symbolically, such a person "withstands the ravages of the storm."

Harold and Louise in a tender moment

TURNING POINTS

Louise Goler-Brittain and Harold D. Brittain III
Silver Spring, Maryland

It's late Friday night. Harold Brittain arrives home, road-weary and eager to see his wife and daughters after another week of work and travel. Louise greets him with a warm hug, trying to hide the stress and fatigue of competing at the office and functioning as a single parent while he's gone.

Relaxing into each other's arms, they fleetingly wonder if their drive to being, doing and having the best is taking too much of a toll on their marriage.

Like many well-educated, highly skilled, ambitious couples, Louise Goler-Brittain and Harold D. Brittain III work hard to achieve the good life. They have impressive careers, a lovely home in the Washington, D.C., suburbs, two bright, beautiful daughters and a schedule that tests their sanity.

The two management consultants, so adept at advising clients on taking care of business, find unexpected challenges in balancing work and home life in a commuter marriage.

Both are with internationally respected management consulting firms: Louise in the worldwide technology group of Booz Allen & Hamilton, Inc.'s metropolitan Washington offices; Harold at Perot (as in H. Ross) Systems, Inc.'s Boston-based consulting division, which keeps him away from home Monday through Friday.

Before they took their vows, Louise and Harold agreed that it was vital for both parents to be present and involved on the home front. But for now, Harold's best chance to build his career means constant travel.

Fueled by a desire to take care of his family, he's aiming for the top of the corporate ladder, doing what it takes to prove himself and build a reputation that will enable him to call the shots in the future.

"I want much more than I had as a child," says Harold, who grew up in a "typical middle-class" home. "I'm struggling, in a sense, to catch up to where I think I should be, I guess, because there are things I haven't achieved."

Louise is understanding and supportive, but disheartened by the imbalance in their lives. While Harold is free to focus on work from Monday through Friday, she has to hustle at work and keep things running at home—by herself. This wasn't the situation that she had envisioned or planned. She's as ambitious as Harold, but the commuter marriage is not only stressful, "it has put me on the 'mommy track,' which has limited my professional development."

She admits she'd like Harold to have more of a presence in rearing Robyn, seven, and Camille, four. Harold is torn between his desire to see his wife and children every day and feeling the pressure to succeed and get to a certain point professionally before he can make a change.

These experts in advising their clients on how to avoid and solve problems know that their love and devotion to each other and the girls are the key to meeting this challenge.

They've overcome past obstacles—several on the road to getting together.

Harold was a new hire at Booz Allen & Hamilton, Inc., where Louise had worked for two years.

He was twenty-five, a year out of Howard University's School of Business, and he had a girlfriend.

She was thirty-four, well traveled and accustomed to dating older, sophisticated men.

He was shy, and assumed that she was married.

She was happily single.

He didn't believe in dating people he worked with. Still, the more he got to know Louise, the more determined he was to win her heart.

And he made a pretty bad first impression.

When Harold started at Booz Allen & Hamilton in September 1987, some buddies had invited him to get together for the Columbus Day holiday. He stopped Louise, a co-worker, in the hallway to ask whether they had the day off.

"The first thing I thought was, 'I don't *believe* this Negro is asking about a day off and he hasn't even been here a week!' " she recalls. She replied with a terse, "No, we don't get it off," and suspected him of being trifling.

Working on the same team, they exchanged office chitchat. Once they discovered their common midwestern roots (she's from Detroit; he's from Cleveland), they started talking regularly. "We realized we were in tune and in sync with each other," Louise says.

On their first evening outing, "We sat down at seven and ordered a drink," Harold says. "When we got up to leave at eleven, we still hadn't finished even that one drink."

"The conversation just flowed; it was very easy, very comfortable," Louise recalls. "I thought, 'Here's somebody I can really talk to.' "

Harold told Louise about his girlfriend and his policy against dating anyone in the workplace, saying, "If we'd met under different circumstances, I'd be interested in you."

As he walked her to her car, she gave him her home number. "Don't lose it. You won't get it again," she warned.

Harold couldn't deny his attraction to Louise. "Here's this beautiful woman with this intellect, and she still has that girl-next-door quality. What excited me beyond the package was her other qualities and characteristics: she was strong and independent, she was directed, she had places in life that she was going. She had a plan. I was impressed by that, and I envisioned that this was the type of woman that I'd eventually settle down with."

Both found their common down-to-earth midwestern values a refreshing change from the status-conscious, cutthroat Washington, D.C., corporate world.

Still, they were not on the same page. While Harold was thinking romance, Louise enjoyed his company but viewed him strictly as a younger friend, someone with whom she could share conversations, meals, perhaps some cultural events.

When Harold later told Louise he had broken up with his girlfriend, she "felt kind of betrayed. I thought, 'He's just like the others—after I say I'm interested in friendship, he wants to push it; he just wants to sleep together.' "

Harold was up-front about his agenda. "If there's something I want, I don't care what anyone says. I am going to pursue it and I am going to obtain it. It's going to be a long day before I throw in the towel. Even when I initially appear to give in, it's because I'm tired, but not exhausted. I'll just regroup and come back with another strategy."

Then he learned her age. Out one night, Louise had to show her driver's license. When Harold, who had guessed that she was about three years older than him, realized the difference was nine years, "I was a little stunned, a little taken aback. I got scared at that moment and thought maybe I should back down or back out.

"Then I thought about it, and realized that it hadn't made any difference. I decided I wouldn't let it intimidate me." He asked Louise whether she wanted their friendship to grow into more.

No, she told him, we aren't going to cross that line.

"The first time we had a serious conversation about the age difference, I tried to explain, 'I'm too old for you. There are things I've done in life—such as traveling internationally and living on my own as an adult—that you haven't had as much experience with,' " Louise says. "I felt I was much more worldly. Even though we'd had a lot of good conversations, there were things we couldn't discuss because he hadn't had the experience."

Then he tried to kiss her. They were at Louise's apartment, enjoying wine, cheese, good music and great conversation. Harold was stressed. "It was my first time at her apartment. I'd wanted to kiss her but hadn't, and was uncertain what to do. I was wrestling with my attraction to her and my policy against dating on the job, along with her insistence that we be 'just friends.' "

Sensing Harold's tension, Louise offered to massage his shoulders. He agreed and, after asking if it was okay, he removed his shirt. Moments later, when he turned to kiss her, she tersely reminded him that they were *friends*.

Frustrated by the mixed messages, Harold told Louise that it was unfair of her to discount their relationship on the basis of age, and went home angry. After he left, Louise said she looked back over her actions and words to see if she had sent the wrong signals. She reviewed the many things she liked about Harold, acknowledged the attraction and "reached a turning point where it was okay for me to start considering him romantically."

Still, she had to overcome her own fears about the age difference. "There were times when I stopped and asked myself what I was doing and whether it made sense. I couldn't confirm it logically, and that's what I like to do. I just figured I was getting involved with

Louise and Harold at their wedding

someone who was immature, plain and simple. I could feel myself being drawn closer and it scared me because I thought I couldn't maintain the control that I had before. I took two steps forward, then one step back."

Louise's older sister, Veta Goler, Ph.D., head of the Drama/Dance department at Spelman College, remembers Louise's ambivalence. "She told me they had these great conversations. Then she wondered whether the generational difference would come up and he wouldn't understand a point of reference. But if there's somebody that your heart just kind of sings for . . ."

Louise's next turning point was the summer of 1988. She was working and going to graduate school at night when her father died after a two-year struggle with cancer. When Harold came from Washington, D.C., to Michigan for the memorial service, "the first traumatic event in my life, I was very much impressed with his support. He was very concerned with my emotional well-being and very much there for me."

By that fall, she and Harold started to discuss marriage, and by Christmas, they were sharing the news with family and friends.

Though they had already agreed to wed, Harold surprised Louise with a formal proposal.

They were married on June 3, 1989, in a traditional ceremony at Washington, D.C.'s Shiloh Baptist Church before about two hundred people, followed by a honeymoon in Ocho Rios, Jamaica.

The early days were easy: they worked together at Booz Allen, ate many of their meals in restaurants and stayed on the fast track at work.

Then Robyn was born in December 1991, shifting Louise's main focus to family and home. The following spring, Harold changed employers and began traveling regularly. After Camille was born in September 1994, he was traveling less. And for eight months in 1997 and 1998, he was local again. This made his eventual return to the road even harder for Louise and the girls.

"It's catching up with me," Harold admits. "I always knew that I wanted to travel for the sake of the work that I've been doing. For a while, I thought it was good for me, 'cause it helped me grow in some of the ways Louise was talking about before we married: things you experience working in different environments. Yet, I realize the need to be more of a stable force for my kids. I want to be there for family meals. I've been looking to try and identify the right spot to land."

Louise concedes that while her independence and organizational abilities help her manage the day-to-day demands well, "I can't handle the girls' reactions to Daddy not being here for a few days. We try to talk with him on the phone most nights. Sometimes he'll call in the morning before they leave for school.

"Weekends are a blur, with errands and the kids' activities. One of the things Harold and I haven't been doing is spending time together. We're trying to address that," she says.

"Sometimes I resent being the sole parent Monday to Friday," Louise says. "I may talk with him about something that's frustrating me and he'll make a suggestion, but I've got to deal with the problem in real time."

They've reached impasses before, and worked to find a way out. In 1995, when "communication between us just broke down," they saw a counselor.

Harold came face-to-face with one of his own contradictions. "There was probably more than I would ever admit, competition between she and I. I think a lot of the challenges I had in the marriage were what I considered Louise to be competing with what I saw as the role that men typically like to assume in the relationship. That was part of her independent spirit that I was attracted to, but later frustrated by because I couldn't manage it. I recognize that she needs more room to branch out and seek out other things that she might want to do with her life, and that I must not be threatened by that."

Counseling helped Louise "learn to be more tolerant. . . . I like to plan things out so that I know what the outcome is going to be. . . . Sometimes you just can't have that level of control." Louise recognizes that "Harold is a wonderful companion who is committed to reaching the goals that we have set. We realize those goals could change. But because we have the friendship and communication, we can say, 'This isn't working for us; let's do something different,' to the point where we recognize we need help and aren't afraid to go and get that help."

"In general, we feel that continuing counseling might be beneficial in resolving uncommunicated frustrations and differences," Harold adds.

There is a beneficial side to Harold's travel. In the late spring of 1994, the whole family (Louise was pregnant with Camille) took a much-needed vacation to Trinidad to spend time with Louise's younger sister and her family. Harold's accumulated frequent flier miles allowed them to fly first-class round trip for a vacation that was a relaxing treat from beginning to end.

Having a family has not changed Louise's ambitions, and her main frustration is not meeting her own professional expectations. "Years back, envisioning our careers, I thought that we'd both do a little traveling as part of our jobs, but not this. . . . I'm the provider and caretaker all week, and when he comes home on the weekends, he's totally drained and looking for me to provide wifely attention, caring and tenderness. And I'm looking for him to give me some relief 'cause I've been with the kids and working. That's been difficult."

In Harold's absence, Louise and the girls have formed their own routines, "and when Harold is home longer than a weekend, it throws the routines off."

He worries that he's odd man out. "I can be sitting right in the room with our daughters and Louise is somewhere else and when they want something, they ask Mommy. You realize how little power you have. . . ."

Having two natural-born leaders in one household presents its own complications. "We have intellectual conversations about traditional male and female roles, who's better at what and letting that person take the lead," Harold says. "But sometimes that's easier said than done. Sometimes neither one of us is willing to concede certain issues."

Despite the hurdles, "We're still here," Louise observes. "What keeps us together is the level of commitment and the fact that, in stressful and nonstressful times, we talk about the things that remind us of why we got together in the first place, how we got through our challenges, how we overcame the obstacles and got to where we are. That's what makes it work for us—the commitment that we made is there through everything."

They agree that the friendship they established in the beginning also holds them together. Tallying the checks and balances of their relationship, they see something worth holding on to.

He makes her feel young, she says, "just by being himself. He is very caring, very loving, very sensitive. I feel a great deal of respect from him; he treats me the way he feels a woman should be treated. I think he puts a lot of effort into making sure that I feel loved so I understand it's coming from his heart."

Harold says he loves Louise's "challenging personality. I like to try to influence her, and it's difficult. That keeps me trying. She's terribly sexy. I don't always tell her, but I think her figure is still as cute, after two kids, as it was when I met her."

He is attracted, too, to her vulnerable side. "I think she's ultrasensitive and there's a protective wall around her. All these years I've been trying to get to that sensitive individual inside."

When Robyn was about two months old, she had surgery for a hernia. Harold says he was surprised when the normally calm, take-charge Louise "broke out in tears and grabbed on to me." In those moments, he feels the sweetness of their interdependence.

Louise says that Harold is the romantic in the family, more apt to engage in discreet public displays of affection than she is, and quicker to show his emotions. She teases and tickles him and he "laughs at my pitiful jokes." On holidays, she likes to spoil him with several cards and gifts throughout the day. He admits that he was "very touched" when she gave him a surprise birthday party.

They have come to view their opposite styles as sources of strength. "When the relationship gets rough, you think about what life would be like if we weren't together. You don't dissolve the partnership because you have differences. You stay in it and if you make it through that storm, it will probably prove to be very good."

The loneliness caused by frequent separations remains the biggest challenge. "I think about him frequently, wonder what he's doing, thinking how he is and how much I miss him," Louise confides.

"Recently, I *pined* for her," Harold says. "I was sitting in the Chicago corporate apartment before I went to work. I just sat there, gazing out the window. I called out her name and said, 'I wish you were here.'"

In lonely moments, Louise recalls the memory that clarifies the force of their love and devotion. "At the moment we were saying our wedding vows, we looked at one another. I really felt as though we were one, like we were the only two people on earth and I was trying to convey how much I loved him and wanted to be married to him forever. I felt that we really connected and that there was total love between us. Afterwards my mother and sister, Linda, said it was as though we were all alone. We really came together as one in that moment."

TABONO

PADDLE (OAR)

This symbol represents the strength, confidence and persistence needed to foster a steady boat in unsure water. To guide and maneuver the boat, the paddler must use power, maintain conviction and posess endurance. These attributes display a person's self-knowledge and self-awareness and the ability to use these attributes in a positive way.

Barbara and Earl Graves are wed.

RICHES OF THE HEART

Barbara and Earl G. Graves
Westchester County, New York

The name and face of Earl G. Graves are icons of Black ambition and achievement. He is Publisher and CEO of *Black Enterprise* magazine, former chairman and CEO of Pepsi-Cola of Washington, D.C., the largest minority-controlled Pepsi-Cola franchise in the United States, and now chairman, Pepsi-Cola Ethic Advisory Board. He is a nationally recognized authority on Black business development, and is in the front lines of the struggle to help African Americans plant, harvest and enjoy the fruits of success.

What many people may not realize is that this business titan's greatest asset is not his driving ambition, keen intelligence, charismatic charm or business savvy, but his loving wife of thirty-nine years. And while devoted to his mission of creating wealth for himself and others, he values their family, with their three sons and a growing brood of grandchildren, above all.

Unlike many women married to super-successful, famous men, the lovely and dignified Barbara Graves does not seek recognition or revel in her status. Instead, her husband says, she is more likely to stay off to the side, quietly observing the goings-on. When the time is right, she may offer a pertinent comment, or privately share her thoughts with Earl.

"She is not caught up in being Mrs. Earl Graves, the boss's wife," he says. "I would go to events and people would say, 'I haven't met your wife.' The average wife comes up front and wants to be taken seriously, but Barbara might be in the back of the room. That is her sense of values—not wanting to beat her own drum." At the same time, he says, "she can hold a conversation with a board chairman and his wife, feeling just as confident as the person she's talking to. And when it's over, she'll tell me whether or not they were real people."

Earl's decision to court and marry Barbara was "the smartest personal and business move of my life," he writes in his book *How to Succeed in Business Without Being White: Straight Talk on Making It in America.* "She has always provided me with a guiding sense of perspective and balance. Her values and principles have kept me on track over the years. It was Barbara who taught me, for example, what true integrity is."

Those lessons began early in their relationship.

Earl was a handsome, debonair Army man, attending Airborne and Ranger School, jumping out of airplanes and full of himself. In college, he joined Omega Psi Phi fraternity (the infamous "Q Dogs") and had an eye for the ladies.

Barbara Kydd was a first-grade teacher, picture-pretty, innocent and content with her work and her life.

Their best friends, Doris and Walter, were dating. When Earl saw a picture of Barbara at Doris's house and asked to meet her, a blind date was arranged.

Barbara wasn't too enthusiastic, but "as a favor to Doris, I consented to meet him." She gave the soldier high marks for his first impression.

"When I opened the door, standing beside Doris and Walter was a tall, pleasing-looking young man in an Army uniform. On closer inspection, as he came in to meet my parents, I noticed that he was spit-shined from head to toe, with a crease in his pants that was as sharp as a razor.

"He was friendly and polite, with a broad open-faced smile that showed beautiful white, gleaming teeth. He extended his hand to my father and my dad commented, amusingly and approvingly, on the firmness of his grip. Obviously, this was the effect Earl wanted to give.

"I liked his bearing—tall, straight and confident—and I liked his large, bright eyes that were penetrating but kind. His enormous hands were beautifully shaped and showed strength without hardness, beauty without softness."

He was drawn to her looks and aura of wholesome modesty. But when, on the first date, Barbara said that she wanted to have thirteen kids, Earl thought, "I'll never see *her* again."

Still, he gave her his telephone number and an invitation to use it. Barbara replied, "I don't call guys," Earl recalls. "I said, 'Clearly this is my last date; she doesn't realize who I am.' I thought that, between being a lieutenant and being an Omega, if I said 'hello' to a lady, she should consider herself lucky to meet me."

When two weeks passed without a word from Barbara, Earl's friend, Walter, said, "I think you're gonna have to call her, Graves."

He called and invited her to his favorite date spot—the parking area at New York's LaGuardia airport. "I had a '55 Buick, and that car knew its way there as well as I did. It was a place where you could relax and have a very nice time sitting in your car with a young lady. Barbara had never been to LaGuardia and she wanted to go. I was roaring out there, whistling to myself. You couldn't tell me I wasn't tough. I thought, 'This is gonna be so easy, it's embarrassing.'" Plus, "Using up two gallons of gas was a whole bunch of spending money for me."

He pulled into his usual spot, in the dark parking area. "She said to me, 'How can we see the planes from here?' I said, 'Did you really think we came all the way out here to *see the airplanes land*?' She looked at me like I was crazy and said, 'I think you'd better start the car, because I cannot see the planes, and I cannot see what you have in mind.'"

Leaving the airport, Earl—who had been "going from one frat party to the next and meeting a different girl each weekend"—began to see the light.

"What meeting Barbara did was make me a different person and change my values," he says. "When you start to miss somebody, you start to think about them, you start to need them. She was innocent, and hadn't been around. In addition, she just had some values. It caused me to stop and think about that."

They saw each other each weekend, when Earl and Walter left the Army base in Fort Dix, New Jersey, to visit their Brooklyn homes.

Earl's manners made a big impression. "He was courtly, in an old-fashioned way, in the way he opened doors for me, walked down the street nearest to the gutter, took his hat off as he entered a home or elevator . . . all the things I had seen my father do," Barbara recalls. "I liked the fact that these precious courtesies were still alive."

Both came from solid, hardworking West Indian immigrant families who had settled in Brooklyn to give their children a shot at the American dream. Barbara, an outstanding student and the first in her family to graduate from college, achieved her childhood goal of becoming a teacher soon after receiving her degree from Brooklyn College. Earl joined the ROTC program while attending Morgan State College (now University.) "After graduation in 1957, I entered the Army, where I attended Airborne and Ranger School and completed my career with the rank of Captain, as a member of the 19th Special Forces Group, the Green Berets," he writes.

While Earl enjoyed the discipline and structure of the military, he had bigger plans for his future. In college, he started a business selling flowers on campus, and "followed the West Indian tradition of working multiple jobs." Still, his announcement that he wanted to go into business was met with shock.

"The concept of being Black and in business was still considered to be almost seditious even when I was a student at [the historically Black] Morgan State . . . from 1953 to 1957," he writes. "My classmates, and some professors, too, were generally incredulous, even scandalized, when I told them my chosen course of study. 'Why are you majoring in business?' they would ask, and with good reason. There were no corporations coming to recruit Black students at that time, and there were no banks lining up to give us loans to start our businesses, nor was there a family business awaiting me back home.

"Still, my response was blunt because I wanted to make it clear that I regarded my future as unlimited, regardless of how anyone else might have felt. 'I want to make a lot of money,' I would respond. 'And I want to create change.' "

But Earl didn't have a specific strategy for achieving his goals. As he shared his dream with Barbara, she helped him see the need to develop a plan. "She pulled me down to earth and let me know this is the real world."

Despite Earl's failed LaGuardia seduction scheme, Barbara was impressed—and smitten.

"Soon it became apparent to me that here was a very special person in my life. He was at ease with my family, and I with his. I began looking forward to weekends just to see him, and began dreading our time apart.

"I loved holding his hand when we walked; loved talking about and sharing all kinds of things with him; loved the long, lingering kisses at the end of each goodnight, and adored the way he looked at me and made me feel so special. It didn't take too long before I realized that these feelings were what we call being in love.

"What made me certain that this was the 'real thing' probably was the fact that I felt that he didn't just love me, but *respected* me. When I expressed my ideas, he really listened to them seriously. I was accustomed to this from my very vocal family, where discussions often shed light as well as heat. I was, after all, a cherished daughter of a loving father and proud mother. But I was also a very naive, very inexperienced young woman, who, as a matter of course, expected that only someone as wonderful as my father would come into my life. As I look back now, I was very lucky."

After eight months of courtship, Earl proposed marriage—and a long engagement.

"When I realized I loved her very much and wanted to get married, I said, 'Let's wait two years,' " Earl recalls, explaining that he had "a lot of ladies" to break the news to. "I figure if I'm not married, then I can still hang out with the guys," he says with a laugh. "She said, 'If we're going to get married, let's get married in six months. I don't believe in long engagements.'

"I thought, 'I don't want to lose this lady, so I'd better make some adjustments.' "

Barbara had a reason for her time line. "While I was as certain as any twenty-three-year-old can be that I was ready for marriage, I wanted to be sure that he, at twenty-four, was, too," she explains. "So I suggested that we keep this proposal and acceptance private. If, in three months, we were still certain of our commitment to each other, we would make a public announcement at an engagement party and then marry six months later. He thought this was odd, but perhaps was secretly relieved to have some wiggle room. It probably also intrigued him and made him determined not to let this odd bird go."

Barbara and Earl had a large, military wedding on July 2, 1960, in St. George's Episcopal Church on Marcy Avenue in Brooklyn. The school year had just ended, and some of Barbara's students came to see their teacher get married. "The colors of the dress uniforms of the Army were incredibly distinct," she recalls. "The jackets were a different color blue from the pants and with gold buttons on the jacket, the men looked more like very proper doormen than officers and gentlemen. I chose a pale yellow for my sister's matron of honor dress (she had married two weeks prior to me) and a complementary pale green for the bridesmaids' dresses.

"My friend Joan's sister made my dress and the other dresses and I made the girls' headpieces. I borrowed my best friend Jeanine's headpiece. I gave myself a manicure, washed and set my own hair and put on my own makeup. I also paid for my wedding. Not unusual occurrences in 1960 in Bedford-Stuyvesant, Brooklyn."

Barbara and Earl spent their wedding night at the Manhattan Hotel in New York City and flew the next morning to Nantucket for a week-long honeymoon. "It was the first time I had stayed in a hotel and the first time I flew in an airplane," Barbara says. "Although I did not know it then, these were just two of many firsts that I was privileged to experience over the next thirty-nine-plus years."

The honeymoon flight was a first for Earl, too, because "we both landed for the first time. Every plane I'd been in up to that point, I'd jumped out of."

Before the marriage, the young couple faced new choices. "Earl was trying to decide if he wanted to make a career of the service or get out," Barbara says, sharing an impression she'd formed during their engagement. "I was invited to Fort Dix for an officers' function, but earlier in the day had participated in a 'hen party' given by a senior officer's wife. Most of the wives were young and appeared to be very timid and too deferential to the hostess. Discussing my impressions with Earl afterward, he said I was right. Some of the senior officers' wives 'pulled rank' on the junior officers' wives—that was the military. I thought about this all week.

"When we saw each other that next weekend, I asked him if he had made a decision about whether or not to stay in the military. He had not, but wanted to know why I asked. It was then that I told him that I would not be a good military wife because I would challenge the expectations of a senior officer's wife. That would probably not bode well for his career. He listened, smiled and said that if the military life didn't suit me, he would get out, since his happiness lay in my happiness. When his time was up, he did leave the military."

"We both knew that we wanted a more open field than a military base in which to run and raise our family," Earl says.

They moved into Earl's mother's house in Brooklyn. He took a job selling real estate and they started their family.

Earl ("Butch") Jr., was born on January 5, 1962. Barbara brought him home four days later—on Earl's twenty-seventh birthday. "Butch was a wonderful baby and I was a very overcautious new mother," Barbara says. "He was well built and showed remarkable physical aptitude, even as a baby. It was not surprising to either of us when Butch developed into a world-class athlete."

John, "a beautiful baby with intense bright eyes that seemed to be all-knowing," came along in May 1963. "He became our 'Philadelphia lawyer,' always challenging and repeating verbatim what we may have said on a previous occasion. Many a day we would privately shake our heads at the sound arguments that this skinny little kid would come up with." As expected, Barbara says, "Johnny became an attorney."

"Two cribs, two high chairs and two children sixteen months apart matures a young couple quickly," she admits. Four years later, Michael was born. "Mike was our biggest baby and it seems as though he went from birth to toddler stage in an instant. His was the shortest baby stage because his brothers prodded him to keep up with them and he was such a loving, darling little boy that we just hung out together while the others were in school. Mike is still the largest of our sons, with the sweetness that brings back memories of the chubby-cheeked cherub who was always by my side."

Earl did so well selling Brooklyn real estate that he sought new challenges. In 1964, he went to the New York State Democratic campaign headquarters and volunteered on the Lyndon B. Johnson–Hubert H. Humphrey presidential campaign. Earl met and impressed Senator Robert F. Kennedy, who soon hired him.

The three years he spent with Senator Kennedy gave him "an education in the use of power and money in this country," Earl writes. "I saw firsthand what sort of freedom could be had with wealth and power. I became even more determined to claim at least some of it."

Earl, who was with Kennedy when he was killed in Los Angeles on June 5, 1968, writes that "the years I spent on his staff have had a lasting impact on me and on how I approach my business and my social responsibilities."

Accepting the offer of a Ford Foundation work-study grant, Earl went to his grandparents' native land of Barbados to study entrepreneurship and economic development. Living in an economically thriving Black country that was controlled mostly by White outsiders, Earl realized that business held more power than government for Black people.

Back in the United States, Earl started a consulting business for Black economic development and joined the board of the Small Business Administration. When he mentioned his dream of starting a newsletter for Black entrepreneurs and corporate managers, SBA director Howard Samuels and others encouraged him to make it a full-fledged magazine.

After consulting with several experts and researching the potential for advertising revenue, *Black Enterprise* magazine was born. It was risky, but Barbara backed Earl all the way. Earl gave the business his all, but even with the demands of a fledgling publication, family was his number one priority. "It was not impossible to work very hard at the business and make it to my sons' little league games."

"Earl has always worked hard professionally, but never put that work before the work of keeping a family connected," Barbara agrees. When the premier issue of *Black Enterprise* came out in August 1970, "our children were eight, seven and three. The commitment to be an active part of our sons' lives has kept Earl involved with them from infancy to today. While his weekday hours were long, weekends were devoted to family, which found us doing special things like playing ball, ice skating, taking a walk, gathering leaves, building a snowman—the building blocks of family memories. He was a fun father, blessed with re-membering the child in himself."

That balance went both ways. Barbara was an integral part of *Black Enterprise* from the start, running every department at the magazine except for sales. "When she wasn't called away to her first duty with the children, she was an extremely active and influential part of the business," he writes. "She worked in the business, she ran editorial at one point and when our chief financial officer died, she learned how to run that until we got a CFO," Earl says with pride. "She has always provided me with a guiding sense of perspective and bal-ance. She watches my back. Anything she was doing, I didn't have to second guess. I could feel a comfort level that it would turn out best for me."

Barbara has always been popular with the staff, he says. "She's a great conversationalist; I'm not. She is a very smart lady, very strong, very opinionated, and the best writer I've ever met. She's our fount of knowledge—what she'll do is cut to the chase of what's right and wrong."

Earl often cites Barbara's strong sense of values and their impact on his life and success. In the early days of *Black Enterprise,* the Graves family was the second to integrate Armonk, New York, where they bought a home. Later, many of the town's mostly White residents objected to a plan to build low-income public housing. Earl had been too preoccupied with business matters to pay much attention to the debate, and when Barbara mentioned the need for them to support the public housing plan, he replied that he had "enough battles in the office."

"We are going to be in this one, too," Barbara said, and she "made sure I got with the program and that the city fathers were informed about where the Graves family stood on the issue," he writes.

Despite their success with *Black Enterprise* and other business ventures, encounters with racism and ignorance sometimes left Earl "exhausted, beaten, bloodied and bruised. No matter how down I've been, she has always raised my spirits, cleaned me up and sent me back into the fray," he writes.

"That's their problem, not yours," Barbara would assure him.

"I was at a board meeting in Belgium and some guy made a reference to 'a nigger in the woodpile.' There were a couple hundred people in the room and I didn't know whether to drape the chair over his head or ignore it. I called her and she suggested I talk with him." As always, Earl took Barbara's advice, and felt better for it.

Barbara is comfortable with her role and contributions. "I never thought that it was a burden to be supportive of a creative, adventurous partner—and partner I was," Barbara says. "It is not immodest to say that I was a very important part of the building of our business. I was the life force that gave him peace of mind and a calm, loving atmosphere to come home to. I was not his competition. I was his support. And a family, like a building, cannot stand without firm support."

On their climb up the ladder of prosperity, the Graveses made sure their boys were firmly grounded. "Together we talked to our sons about the real world—the communities we lived in over the years, the kind of country we lived in, the extended Black community that we were a part of and the political, economic and social impact of it all," Barbara reflects. "As they matured, our conversations deepened to their responsibilities to become educated, aware and involved."

They set an example—by sharing with family members in need and embracing philanthropy with gifts such as the $1 million donation they made to Morgan State University.

Among their blessings, Earl says, is the fact that all three sons "are key players in my business ventures." After graduating from Yale University and fulfilling his childhood dream of playing in the NBA with the Philadelphia 76ers, Milwaukee Bucks and Cleveland Cavaliers, Earl ("Butch") Jr., earned an MBA from Harvard and is now president and chief operating officer of Earl G. Graves Publishing. Johnny, a graduate of Yale Law School, is president of Black Enterprise Unlimited, which develops and markets events and products that support and expand the Black Enterprise brand. And Michael, after graduating from the University of Pennsylvania, went on to head up the family's Pepsi-Cola bottling franchise in Washington, D.C., which he continues to run.

Despite phenomenal success, international acclaim, numerous honors, prestigious board appointments and dozens of honorary degrees, Earl and Barbara agree that a loving family is the truest indication of achievement. "We taught our sons that marriage is sacred and let's get it right the first time," Earl says.

It appears that all three sons got that lesson right. "Butch and Roberta are the parents of four children—twin girls, Erika and Kristin, and two boys, Earl (Gibby) III and Theodore," Barbara says. "Johnny and Caroline are the parents of two children—a girl, Veronica and a boy, Carter. Mike and Kymberly are the new parents of baby girl Melanie."

Though their sons are grown, the Graveses get together often, enjoying travel, ski trips, multigenerational Super Bowl parties, annual African American football classics and visits to their beach homes in Sag Harbor, New York.

But Earl and Barbara also cherish their one-on-one time. They enjoy furnishing their homes, sharing Christmas shopping and just being in each other's company. To fan the flames of romance, they check into a New York City hotel for a five- or six-day date. "That means I treat her the same way as when I was courting her," Earl says with a chuckle. "I don't discuss the company, and we are always holding hands."

Reflecting upon their relationship, Earl says, "I think that being married thirty-nine years is a refinement of process. You work at it every day." Part of that work involves give-and-take. Earl accompanies Barbara to the theater, where he's been known to fall asleep. "And if I said to her I want to go whitewater rafting, she says, 'Okay. Is there a way to meet you at the other end of the river?'"

When they do disagree, Earl says, it usually takes Barbara a couple of days "to get over it. I usually say, 'I forgive you. I know you made a mistake. I know you're getting older or the moon was out last night.' And we both laugh. It takes humor," he says. "And then when it's over, it's over. She says, 'You didn't listen to me again.' " Earl admits he's "still learning to listen."

Barbara is philosophical about their contrasts. "Earl and I are very different in personality. He is very sociable, gregarious and full of mischievous fun. I am more reserved, happy with small-scale social interactions, and enjoy quiet time alone, preferably with a good book. But this characterization is not the only identification of each of us. Earl, of course, has a very serious side, which comes out in his business dealings, and I enjoy a good belly laugh as much as anyone. The balance of all these things is key to a healthy relationship.

"We always found time for each other—when the kids were young, when the business was in its most intense earliest days and today. Earl never forgets an important date in our lives and often, even today, will send me flowers or a note 'just because I love you.'

"His kindness, tenderness and romantic spirit nurtures my soul and inspires me to be a better person. Earl's inexhaustible energy is put forth for a friend, a relative, a colleague—it is the only way he knows how to do anything. Special things are always being thought up, planned and executed with a precision of excellence that is his trademark. But more importantly, they are done in an atmosphere of love and caring."

"I think you have to work at it, you have to plan it, you have to make up your mind you're going to make time for each other," Earl says. "We were always doing things we could share together."

"We are lucky with our sons," Barbara says. "They are good friends to each other, accomplished young men, contributing members of society, loving husbands and devoted fathers. What I hope we showed them by example of our love and marriage is that you can disagree (as Earl and I certainly do on ways to approach things), but the person you take on as a life partner must share some fundamental values. A pretty face must be attached to a sensitive soul and an intelligent mind in order for marriage to work."

In reflecting upon her family's success, Barbara is passionate about the emotional investment that a healthy family requires.

"Because I don't hold myself up as a role model for anyone, I hesitatingly implore young Black families to postpone some of the ephemeral things that they think they cannot do without and embrace some of the more substantive gifts of life. As an observer of my own children and their peers, I am amazed and saddened by some of the things I see among many of the most highly educated, professionally successful young couples in our Black community. Having more and more 'things' for themselves and their children, rising to the 'top' of wherever they are climbing and employing a 'nanny' as a substitute parent have become status symbols of having arrived.

"The pain for me is that these very privileged young couples don't have a clue that they have not even begun the journey, let alone arrived. The most precious persons in their lives are their children, who must be given time with their parents . . . time to read books, to tell family stories, to listen to thoughts being developed, to sit quietly or cuddle and laugh. Not 'quality time,' as the people who are hyping the rushed minutes that too-busy parents are giving their children call it. Time. Parental time. The only significant thing, along with love, that we can give our children. Perhaps it will also be the most rewarding experience that a parent will ever feel."

1st row, seated:
Earl G. Graves, Sr., and Theodore
2nd row, left to right:
Earl III, Barbara Graves with Carter, Veronica and twins Erica and Kristin
Third row, left to right:
Roberta, Earl Jr. (Butch), Kymberly, Caroline, John and Michael

The potential that the cocky paratrooper and the down-to-earth schoolteacher saw in each other on a blind date has become a life of personal and professional riches.

Barbara and Earl Graves know that love is the sweetest fuel for life's journey. What makes theirs work, he says, "is our faith in each other. And my need for her. I call her during the day. She calls me during the day. You really do have to share—what makes us love each other is the sharing."

Whether representing the face of Black business success or grinning from the midst of their growing brood on the family Christmas card, Earl is quick to credit the lovely Barbara for being his anchor and guiding light. "When I look at her, I feel love and appreciation for her value." At an age where some of their friends' spouses are dying, "I can't imagine life without her."

Barbara says that she has "been blessed with receiving this abundance of joy because he never takes our love for granted. Nor do I."

BESE SAKA

BUNCH OF COLA NUTS

A symbol of affluence, power, abundance, plenty, togetherness and unity. Cola nuts used to be one of the most important cash crops in Ghana. Cola trade was one of the three major items of the early trade in the Gold Coast area, along with salt and gold, and has been a very important part of Ghana's economic history.

AT THE END OF THE DAY

Alma and Colin Powell
McLean, Virginia

Some thought it was a moment of purely political significance. But to many, it was one of the most loving tributes ever publicly paid to a Black woman by her man.

When General Colin L. Powell announced in 1995 that he would not consider running for president of the United States, he explained that his decision was based partly on the fact that he didn't hunger for the power or prestige of the Oval Office, and partly on the lack of fire in his belly for the battlefield of presidential politics. However, the presence of the elegantly beautiful woman at his side told another, more personal, side of the story. When the general turned to his wife, Alma, and acknowledged that her reluctance to see him run had been a major factor in his decision, the heart of many African American women who have loved Black men leapt in joyous understanding.

"For the past few weeks, I have been consulting with friends and advisers," he said at the November 8 press conference. "I have spent long hours talking with my wife and children, the most important people in my life, about the impact an entry into political life would have on us. It would require sacrifices and changes in our lives that would be difficult for us to make at this time. The welfare of my family had to be uppermost in my mind."

All of the reasons that Colin Luther Powell, the Harlem-born, Bronx-reared son of Jamaican immigrants, should *not* seek to become the epitome of the American Dream were embodied in his strong-hearted, soft-spoken wife of thirty-three years.

Like most African Americans, Alma lived with the ambivalence of wanting her husband to soar to the highest heights and the fear of the potentially disastrous results. The Birmingham, Alabama, native knew the horrors of lynchings. She had been in the 16th St. Baptist Church in Birmingham where, on September 15, 1963, four young girls were killed by a bomb planted by the Ku Klux Klan. As Colin rose through the ranks of the U.S. military to become the first Black Chairman of the U.S. Joint Chiefs of Staff, she understood that his growing popularity was a double-edged sword with the potential to cut a painful swath through their lives. When the rallying cry rose for him to blaze through history to lead the nation, memories of the assassinations of Medgar Evers, Martin Luther King, Jr., and Malcolm X reminded her of the price that Black leaders are forced to pay all too often.

Alma Powell spoke openly to the media. She described her fear that "crazy people out there" might hurt or kill him if he dared to try for the presidency. He was, she reminded the public, a Black man in America, after all.

Perhaps if she had listened to her first mind years earlier, she wouldn't have faced such a dilemma. Alma Vivian Johnson had not planned to fall in love with, and certainly never intended to marry, a military man.

She came from a well-educated, solidly middle-class family. Her father, Robert C. "R.C." Johnson was the principal of one of Birmingham's two Black high schools, and her uncle, George Bell, was principal of the other. Her mother, Mildred Johnson, was a leader in Black Girl Scouts and at the national level of the Congregational Church. Alma loved music and, after graduating from Fisk University in Nashville, returned to Birmingham to host a radio program, *Luncheon with Alma,* where she spun R&B hits, and occasionally indulged her passion for progressive jazz.

Feeling stifled in her hometown, she went to Boston to study audiology. One winter day in 1961, Alma's roommate Jackie invited her on a double date with her beau Michael and a friend of his. "I do not go on blind dates," Alma fumed, repeating her longtime rule, "and I definitely don't go on blind dates with *soldiers*. How do I know who's going to walk through that door?"

Finally, Alma agreed to go, but not without finding a way to express her displeasure. She replaced her classy look with an uncharacteristically wild ensemble and made herself up like a vamp. Peeking out to see her date, she was shocked to see the shy, baby-faced soldier who appeared so much younger than the men she usually dated. His innocence prompted her to change outfits and return her hair and makeup to their normal state.

Colin was immediately enchanted by the emerald-eyed, ginger-haired beauty. Taking in her alluring figure and graceful moves, he decided that this blind date—his first—"might just work out."

Over drinks and music, they talked. Or, as he describes in his autobiography, *My American Journey,* "Alma did talk, most of the evening, while I listened, entranced. After almost exclusive exposure to girls with New Yawky voices, I was much taken by this soft-spoken Southerner. At one point, she put a question to me natural enough in that era of compulsory military service: How much time did I have left in the Army? Young men she knew went into the service and got out as soon as possible; they could practically tell you how many minutes they still had to serve. I was not getting out, I told her; I was *career* military. She looked at me as if I were an exotic specimen."

By evening's end, she concluded that he was "simply the nicest person I had ever met."

In some ways, it was a case of "opposites attract."

She was, her husband writes, "a well-bred girl from a proper Southern family" whose father viewed Caribbean immigrants with distaste. His folks were "nosy, noisy, fun-loving West Indians" who had studiously avoided the American South and everything associated with it.

She had been an outstanding student, skipping grades and graduating from college at nineteen. He had been a "happy-go-lucky kid, amenable, amiable and aimless," whose ambitious parents worried over his lack of academic commitment.

She was adventurous and goal-oriented. He was a late bloomer who switched majors his first year of college, then discovered his purpose in life when he joined the Reserve Officers Training Corps (ROTC).

She loved the intricate, unpredictable rhythms of progressive jazz and the sweetly seductive tones of R&B. He adored Calypso, with its percolating steel drums and bawdy lyrics. She could tear up a dance floor. His two left feet defied the myth that all Black folks can dance.

They seemed to be meant for each other. Though that's not how he saw it at the time.

A month into their relationship, Colin invited Alma to a New Year's Eve party in his family's New York home. She effortlessly charmed the jovial clan and passed his doting Aunt Beryl's fierce inspection. Colin was surprised when Aunt Beryl announced to the family that the courtship could proceed, even if poor Alma was not Jamaican. "I did not know it was a courtship. I just thought I had a new girlfriend and we were dating. What an idiot," he wrote.

Alma fit in well with his friends, especially the married Army couples. The lovebirds soon became inseparable. Still, Colin was "oblivious to what was happening. I was in love, but I thought it would clear up."

In 1962, he received his orders for South Vietnam. He was excited about going to war, eager to test his training in the heat of battle. When he called Alma with the news, she was not enthused. He drove to Boston to convince her to see his point of view. He was finally getting the chance to really be a soldier. Moreover, he was getting a promotion.

"What does that mean for us?" she asked.

He'd be in Vietnam for a year, with no idea what might happen after that, he answered, adding that he cared deeply for her and would write often.

"I'm not going to write to you," she informed him. If he wanted her for a pen pal, they could call it quits. At age twenty-four, she did not plan to wait around for a maybe.

Devastated, he drove the thirty miles back to the military base at Fort Devens, his mind and heart in a whirl. He lay awake that night reviewing Alma's considerable charms and their feelings for each other. The next day, he returned to Boston to propose.

And though he offered no ring, she said yes.

They were wed on August 25, 1962, at the Congregational Church in Birmingham. Four months after the wedding, Alma was pregnant and Colin prepared to ship off to Vietnam. She took his departure, two days before their first Christmas, in stride. While Alma had never planned to be a military wife, Colin says he knew then that she would "make the perfect life partner for this soldier."

The war kept them apart for a year. She moved in with her parents in Birmingham. Each wrote letters full of love and support, sparing details of the chaos around them. He downplayed descriptions of the dangers he faced from the Viet Cong. She omitted news of the anti–civil rights violence that forced her father to spend sleepless nights with a shotgun across his knees ready to guard his growing family. The newlyweds weathered their separation with affirmative messages of caring and concern.

Colin was in Vietnam when their son, Michael, was born, though he was present for the births of Linda two years later and Annemarie five years after that. Always stoic and calm, Alma kept her family on track through war, peace, Colin's rapid ascension up the military ladder and numerous moves from one Army base to another.

Colin remained as dedicated a family man as he was a soldier, the well-being of his wife and children always uppermost in his mind. As much as he loved serving his country, he was always eager to return home.

Maximizing the role of military spouse, Alma became deeply involved in various types of volunteer work, from churches to women's groups to helping younger officers' wives learn the ropes. What some might consider a sacrifice, she viewed as an investment in her husband's rising career and her family's stability amid the exciting chaos of their lives. The woman who had once shunned military men made her own imprint on the U.S. Armed Forces. Through twenty-two relocations (including one overseas) and Colin's nonstop promotions and opportunities, such as the chance to serve as a White House Fellow, Alma was not only an outstanding wife and mother, but an inspiring role model and teacher to other military wives. In her they saw an example of marriage as partnership. They learned the importance of being resilient and the value of embracing change, even when it was thrust upon them.

Maintaining her sense of style and confidence, Alma offered the general the right mix of loving support and clear-eyed reality checks. When he bragged to her about one of his achievements, she remarked, "That's nice, but I always expect the best of you anyway."

Their devotion to each other manifests itself in matters large and small. When Alma was diagnosed with depression, Colin remained at her side. Throughout the Persian Gulf War, she welcomed him home from long, stressful nights at the Pentagon with hot homemade soup on the stove.

Recalling their thirtieth anniversary celebration in 1992, Colin wrote that "in the lottery of love and marriage, I knew that I had been the big winner."

Since he retired in 1993, they delight in spending time together. But on Colin's first day of civilian life, he experienced a bit of culture shock. Accustomed to being served by his staff, the man who had earned military honors and been honored by heads of state around the world informed his wife that he was ready to eat lunch.

She shot him an I-don't-*think*-so look and lovingly invited him to fix it himself. He pulled a baseball cap down over his eyes and, praying that no one in his affluent suburb recognized him, drove to the nearest fast-food joint.

Today, the Powells are pouring themselves into public service. Having successfully reared their three children—Michael is now an attorney and father of two, Linda an actress and Annemarie an assistant producer for ABC Television—Alma and Colin have set their sights on helping America's youth. The general is heading America's Promise—The Alliance for Youth, serving on a handful of boards and spreading the gospel of volunteerism as one of the country's most requested speakers. Alma is active on charitable boards and a driving force in the Best Friends Program, which provides teenage girls with positive options to sexual activity and early pregnancy.

When asked what he feels is important in life, the general becoms passionate. "What are you gonna do to save the Black community?" he all but commands. "Are you touching just one child? Don't tell me how to save all the Black children, just go out and get *one*. Are you sponsoring a Boys and Girls Club? Do you care what's happening in your school? Are you spending enough time with your children? Are you helping your extended family? So the whole thing comes down to what we all need to do in rebuilding those family values. And I mean that in the home, in the community, in the nation.

"And it really, really starts in the home. And two people getting married. I talk about marriage a lot. People say, 'What's the one institution we have to fix?' It's marriage. Two people ought to get married with the understanding that they intend for it to be a lifelong commitment, and that they will raise children within marriage, and that these children will receive values that essentially are brought to the marriage like genes and chromosomes come together. We've got to start teaching these children that they are ladies, young ladies . . . then we have to work on the young gentlemen. That's a harder sell."

If there is a legacy to be left by his life's work, he says, "I just hope they say, 'He was a pretty good guy, he raised three good children, he had a good marriage.' "

When Colin made the decision about what many consider his greatest opportunity—the chance to lead his country and the free world—his wife's desires were always part of the equation. At the press conference, she explained that the decision "was one that we reached together, as a team, as we have for thirty-three years."

As the Powells have watched their family grow, their fame balloon and their fortunes multiply, their love and devotion continue to serve as both bedrock and guiding light. She knows that her warrior-man will be there, no matter what, with a love as reliable as it is fierce, as tender as it is powerful. He continues to rely upon her calm intelligence, loving counsel and enduring support. Amid the hectic pace and glamour of public life, the once unlikely couple never loses sight of the passion that took them from a blind date to everlasting love. As Michael said when *People* magazine declared his parents one of the greatest love stories of the century, "Through all the fog, at the end of the day, they still look for each other."

AGYINDAWURU

THE GONG OF AGYIN, THE FAITHFUL SERVANT

A symbol of faithfulness, alertness and dutifulness. Agyin was a servant to the King of Asante. Oral accounts say that he was very faithful, gracious and courteous and displayed a readiness to serve.

Laura and Norman's 1947 wedding

A PROMISE MADE, A PROMISE KEPT

Laura Lynem Rates and Norman Rates
Decatur, Georgia

On Saturday, June 21, 1997—a half century to the day after their wedding—Laura Lynem Rates and the Reverend Doctor Norman Rates gathered with family and friends, at Spellman College, which had long been their workplace and home, to celebrate the keeping of the promise they had made so many years before.

"Some people ask us how it feels to be married fifty years," Norman says.

"Yes," Laura adds, "young people can't comprehend how you've been married to the same person for fifty years and still have the love and a concern and caring for each other."

"I'm thankful that I have not had any unhappiness at all in those fifty years," she says. "Some people feel that you have to have some crisis in your relationship to make you closer to each other or stronger. I guess maybe it's because of the way we started out. When we got married, we said we would never discuss divorce."

"We committed ourselves to a lifetime," Norman says. "There was a commitment to God also—that a promise made is a promise to be kept."

Laura and Norman were wed eleven days after they graduated from college, in a traditional ceremony at St. Paul AME Church in Lexington, Kentucky. Laura's father, an AME minster and presiding elder, gave her away.

Norman, who had received a full scholarship at the Lincoln University in Pennsylvania Seminary, remembers, "I had nothing to offer her of a material nature. I had no source of income . . . nothing much to offer her except the assurance that I was a good man and I'd be a good husband."

In a wedding-day letter to his bride, Norman wrote:

> *We'll soon belong to each other for life. You'll be mine and I'll be yours. We'll both be God's. Let us never forget that. Whatever belongs to the one of us belongs to the other and all belongs to God: happiness, sorrow, sickness, health. Let's share it all together.*
>
> *I love you with all my heart. Trust and have faith in me and yourself and I'll do likewise. Encourage me in all my efforts. Correct, don't scold me. Support me. On God and you I'll depend for things that no one else or no other thing can furnish me.*
>
> *I love you, my Little One. Pray for us and our successes in life together. I love you.*

Norman informed Lincoln University officials that they would have to make provisions for his new bride. They hired her to run the campus post office and bookstore for $90 a month. Since married couples could not live in dorms, the newlyweds had to rent a furnished room off campus where they squeezed into a twin bed..

With little money, Norman says, "we had to accept each other on faith" and rely on each other for nearly everything. "We started in what you might call 'material poverty,' " Norman says. "And from that moment on, we always shared; financial things as well as burdens and joys and sorrows. All of those things."

Together they discussed whether Norman should pastor a church or become a college minister (they agreed on the latter). They talked about their plans to have four children, though they were married seven years before Sondra was born, and Shari came seven years later. They had no television, so they listened to music and sports (especially the newly integrated Brooklyn Dodgers) on the radio.

Their pleasures were simple: taking the bus to Philadelphia to go to the movies, dining at little Italian restaurants, spending a day in New York. They split everything—from the price of movie tickets to sandwiches.

The Rateses spent summers working as missionaries (for one salary) to agricultural migrant workers in rural New York State. Norman worried about his "innocent little Kentucky girl being around such rough conditions." Though some were tough, Laura never considered leaving. Looking back, she says the experience helped her grow.

Laura Lynem, the baby girl of five children, was born into a farming family outside Cynthiana, Kentucky, near Lexington. Dissatisfied with farming, her father became a minister in the AME Church. Laura lived a sheltered life, rich with achievement. She was high school class president and winner of an oratorical contest that awarded her a trip to New York City.

Her life changed drastically during her senior year when her mother was killed and Laura was injured in an auto accident. She lost interest in college, but her father insisted that she go so she could take care of herself.

Norman was one of eleven children in an industrious working-class family in Owensboro, Kentucky. His dad worked full-time and ran a successful plumbing business on the side. One of the first in his family to attend college, Norman was popular on campus. He played the field, not expecting to marry until he was about thirty-five, with a house, a car and a good job. But a vision of loveliness changed his plans.

During freshman week at Kentucky State College in Frankfort, Kentucky, Laura strolled past one of the men's dorms, sad and withdrawn. Norman, looking out of an upstairs window, spied the young beauty and whistled in appreciation. She turned her head away and kept walking.

Seeing Laura around campus, he didn't think he had a chance with her. Everything about them was so different, including his working-class and her more middle-class background, and each was seeing someone else. "We started just walking together and talking. Then, all of a sudden, I didn't have a boyfriend and he didn't have a girlfriend," Laura says. "And we found that we wanted to be together."

During Christmas in their junior year, he realized she was his "ideal woman" and proposed on the steps of the old capitol building in Frankfort. Less than two weeks after graduation, they wed.

The Rateses' marriage has been characterized by togetherness. They've done nearly everything in tandem, including work for the same employers. In college they shared a major—sociology—although Laura minored in history and Norman in economics. They cook and clean side by side. She sleeps snuggled into his left shoulder, comforted by his heartbeat.

They keep in shape together—walking in the mall near their home outside of Atlanta. She taught him to swim, he taught her to play tennis and, until recently, they did both together. She doesn't share his passion for football, and he doesn't care for the ballet that she loves, but they enjoy the symphony and theater. Before Laura retired from Spelman in 1995 they strolled the campus daily, hand in hand. They've always shared a car, driving to and from work together, every day. They read each other's thoughts, finish each other's sentences.

So much togetherness, Norman admits, "would kill some people. But it works for us—we're dependent upon each other in a positive sense."

It is such a trademark that some folks panic when they don't see the Rateses together. Once, when they were unable to sit together in their usual church pew, one young lady told her mother that "something must be wrong." The mother called her sister in Maryland (whose wedding Norman had assisted in performing) to relay the news. Laura had to call the mother and her sister to assure them that everything was fine.

The Rateses describe themselves as "totally in sync." Yet, Laura observes, "we are so different." She is proper and reserved; he is a gregarious jokester. She tells the truth with no sugar-coating; he is the essence of diplomacy.

Laura admits she's more intense and prone to worry, especially about the welfare of her family. Once, she was so upset about how someone treated Norman that she developed vertigo. "Don't let anybody hurt my husband or my children," she warns. "I might let it go for a while, but if you continue . . ."

"She's the firebrand," Norman says. "If it was left up to me I would say, 'Down, girl!' "

One difference that has special meaning to Norman is that she is left-handed and he is right-handed. "This is minor," Laura remarks.

"But the minor things are the ones that can cause more trouble," Norman responds, admitting that it took him a while to adjust to the different ways they put the toilet tissue on the roll. He fought the urge to try and change her. "I had to learn that her way of doing things was different from mine and was therefore not wrong. I changed from seeing what she was doing as wrong to seeing it as what she was doing. I had to come to the realization that I would never change it and learn to respect the fact that she did it her way."

He also had to accept that she's a faster walker. On their mall walks, she moves with shorter, more rapid steps and won't slow down to keep pace with him. "I wave at him or pat him as I pass, and keep going," she says with a smile. "I find that irritating," he admits, preferring to walk at the same pace. The difference that may be most significant, given Norman's status as a man of the cloth, is that they are "poles apart" in the ways they relate to God. While he is deeply religious in the formal sense, she describes herself as "more spiritual," praying in her own way and time, and reading for inspiration such works as *The Prophet* by Kahlil Gibran.

Laura feels her beliefs are best expressed "by treating people the way they should be treated, being concerned about things like children, family life, our young people, our young Black males. . . ." She spends hours each week rocking babies in her arms at Grady Hospital in Atlanta.

They have never had a big argument, they say, though it is not unusual for them to disagree. When they do, they talk, realizing that it may take a while to come to a compromise. "But we never go to bed in the heat of anger," Laura says.

If they do, Norman says with a grin, he enjoys a romantic make-up "around two or three in the morning."

"That other business has to be straightened out before," Laura admonishes, giving his hand a firm pat.

Most important, they say, is they have honored their premarital promise never to bring up—or even allow themselves to think—the word "divorce." Each considered their parents' long, loving marriage the standard to emulate.

Their daughters—both single—view their parents as part of a bygone era and doubt that they'll find men as honest, loving and devoted as their father in today's world. Norman and Laura agree that it's a long shot, and advise their daughters to look beyond the surface for the qualities that make a good mate. He may be older, they say, or someone who has been married before. "We tell them that you have to look for somebody different than what you think you need. He may not be a college graduate. Look at a blue-collar person."

After all, they were from different class strata and, after fifty years, say they are more in love than ever. They kicked off their fiftieth anniversary celebration in a sparkling, semiformal gathering at Spelman College, where Norman has served for forty-three years—thirty-nine as college minister, forty-two as chair of the Department of Religion and now as associate chair of the Department of Philosophy and Religion, teaching all the while—and where Laura worked part-time in the Registrar's Office for thirty-five years and now volunteers in the Camille Cosby Center museum.

Fiftieth anniversary kiss

On their fiftieth anniversary, they basked in the tributes of family and friends on the Spelman campus, where they had lived from their arrival in 1954, rearing their daughters in family living quarters fashioned at various dormitories, until they moved to their Decatur, Georgia, home in 1972.

The celebration continued Sunday, June 22, 1997, at Atlanta's First Congregational

United Church of Christ, spiritual home to many of the city's most influential movers and shakers, and where Norman serves as a member of the ministerial team. At the Rateses' request, Spelman President Emerita, Dr. Johnnetta Cole, was the invited guest speaker.

Laura and Norman's fiftieth wedding anniversary celebration in 1997

I cannot tell you how much, Reverend Rates and Laura, I love and respect you. . . . I respect so much the way you practice continuity and change. I know that when you received your early Christian instruction, there wasn't nothin' in there 'bout no equality 'twixt womenfolk and menfolk. But you found in that Christian instruction the kernel of truth and you held on to it. [And] you changed some parts that you had every reason to believe the Good Lord wanted you to change.

The Reverend Doctor Dwight Andrews, senior minister at First Church and a renowned musician, musicologist and composer—who had set the tone for the service and brought tears to folks' eyes with an impromptu saxophone rendition of "My Funny Valentine"—officiated over the renewal of the vows. The Reverend Andrew Young, former ambassador to the United Nations and ex-mayor of Atlanta, presided as the Rateses exchanged their original wedding rings along with two new rings to mark their joyous marital milestone.

Many in the congregation marveled at the longevity of Laura and Norman's romance, their enduring passion and obvious enjoyment of each other.

"Our love is born out of time, and trials and sharing," Norman reflected later. "It is also written in respect for one another. I think how fortunate I am to have a person such as Laura as my wife."

"I'm the one who's fortunate," she responds, caressing his hand.

"I think that our marriage has kept me alive," he says. "And it does make my heart go bumpity-bump." He smiles, casting a long gaze upon her slender, shapely legs.

After five decades, "it's a different kind of love," Laura says. "There are times that, if I think about it or if I look at him for some reason, tears can come to my eyes because of my love for him. Because he's been a good husband and he's been a good father."

"Some people get married to try it out and not to be committed," Norman laments. "We made that commitment to one another in the presence, in the eyes, of God."

A commitment that has proved to be as good, and as solid, as gold.

To Laura

Tender and fresh,
Wakens my love
In softer flesh
This feather of love.
Wide eyes inform me
Dawn has emerged
Kisses me lightly
Make my life surge.
Smiles of devotion
Stretch over my frown
Rapturous emotions
Swirl midst my arms.
Soft tones remind me
Daylight's approach,
But evening will find me
With you, dear, encroached.

Love, Norman

NSOROMA

A CHILD OF THE HEAVENS, STAR

A symbol of faith and the belief in patronage and dependency on a supreme being. Nsoroma symbolizes a person of exemplary character, while representing faith and the idea of hope.

Neil and Jane at their wedding

A PERFECT MATCH

Jane A. Seaberry and Cornelius F. Foote, Jr.
Dallas, Texas

Aweek before Mother's Day 1996, Jane Seaberry lay in a Minnesota hospital, racked with pain and worry, far from her Dallas home. Her husband, Neil Foote, and their three-year-old daughter, Alex, were at her side to hear the doctors' news: the kidney Jane had received via transplant at that same hospital months earlier had failed.

Jane needed another kidney right away. She could go on hemodialysis while awaiting a donor but without a new kidney, she would die.

None of Jane's other relatives were suitable donors, and since doctors traditionally check blood kin first, Neil hadn't been tested. She began dialysis treatments, uncertain of the future, feeling sorry for Neil, who had lost his father a few months earlier and his mother years before. She worried that the sight of her in the hospital again, with tubes coming out of her body, would be hard on little Alex, too.

Neil had only one thought: to save the woman he loved and preserve his family. As the doctors searched frantically for a potential donor, he quietly asked, "What about me?"

The doctors raced through the tests and found that the couple was a match. When Neil told Jane he would be the donor, she recalls feeling "elated at his love and devotion, but concerned that the surgery would be a strain" on his health, and a risk that might leave Alex without either parent. Neil was nervous, but determined.

On Mother's Day, two days after the transplant, Neil jokingly told Jane that she had already received her gift from him. She smiled her agreement.

Along with her gratitude, Jane felt some guilt. She felt okay about going through the operation herself, but didn't feel Neil should have to experience it. "And then he ended up having to have surgery, and this huge scar," she says.

Those things didn't concern Neil. "It was a crisis and I thought, 'I have to rally around the family. That's the meaning of a family.' "

Nearly a year later, Neil, Jane and Alex enjoy a laid-back Sunday morning in their suburban Dallas home. Amid the lovely furnishings and colorful artworks, Neil makes waffles and Jane keeps tabs on Alex, five, who is practicing headstands nearby.

All three look healthy, happy and contented. Their bright eyes and serene faces show no signs of the medical tribulations they have endured over the years.

At age fifteen, Jane learned that she was diabetic. The doctors told her that meant daily insulin shots and no chance of ever having children. Jane took the news in stride, never dreaming she'd someday meet a man who would reverse those predictions.

In 1986 she was a reporter in the business section of the *Washington Post*: "I was young and single, surrounded by other young, single women. Word spread that this 'real cute guy' was coming in to interview for a job. We all gathered around looking at his résumé." Jane, who was thirty-one at the time, saw the "real cute guy" was only twenty-six and hence "a baby." "Forget it!" she thought.

When Neil showed up for his interview, Jane noticed all the women checking out the handsome newcomer, who had a reputation as someone to watch in the newspaper world. He was hired as a reporter in the business section, where he and Jane were among the few persons of color. Neil, impressed with Jane's intelligence and sophisticated demeanor, asked her to lunch.

Jane thought, "Oh, this kid is hitting on me. But he *seems* nice. . . ."

Lunches progressed to movie and dinner dates, and they felt the click of compatibility. Besides work, they had lots in common. Both were from well-educated, professional families and each had spent time in Europe—Jane had gone to school in London and Neil had studied in Spain. They both drove gray Hondas and loved the same Ernest Hemingway books—*The Sun Also Rises* and *A Farewell to Arms.*

"We had great conversations," Neil remembers. "And we seemed comfortable together. It just felt right."

Jane, who loved to entertain, invited Neil to a dinner party at her home. He wowed the gathering with an impromptu post-dinner concert on Jane's piano, then impressed her by volunteering to stay after everyone left to help her clean up.

After Neil washed the dishes, he and Jane looked through her photo albums. They edged toward each other, and Jane thought with relief that, after three months of dating without even a kiss, "the kid" was finally making his move. Neil shocked her by getting up to leave, reminding her that he had a long drive home.

"This was sort of a turning point for me," Jane says. "It was unusual to find a guy who would just want to stay and clean up your house and then leave." She was impressed with his restraint. "He was just the nicest, nicest man I had ever met."

Soon after they began dating, Neil's mother was diagnosed with cancer. On Mother's Day 1987, she went into the hospital. Neil drove from Washington to New York nearly every weekend to see his mom. Many times, Jane went with him. Before she died, Neil's mom said of Jane, "I can tell she loves my son."

They dated for four years. Though Jane and Neil didn't announce any future plans, their friends privately agreed that the two were perfect for each other. They noted how Jane had become less reserved and more apt to crack a joke, and that Neil seemed more focused and grounded than he had in the past.

While their five-year age difference was never a big issue, Jane occasionally wondered about Neil's intentions. "There was a story in the paper about a thirty-five-year-old woman who was single and hadn't found a man," she says. "Neil was reading this story and just laughing his head off about how this woman was thirty-five and couldn't get married. He just thought it was so funny.

"I said, 'What's funny about *that*? I'm thirty-five and I'm not married. We've been dating four years! And it looks like I'm not getting married,' " she recalls.

Neil remembers that "the longer we dated, quite naturally, the more frequently we talked about what was 'taking me so long.' "

As more of their friends married, expectations intensified. But Neil would not be rushed. "My feeling was that it would not do us any good for me to just say we were going to get married because all of our other friends were or because we had been dating too long."

In the fall of 1987, Neil received a frantic call from one of Jane's friends, saying Jane had been hospitalized after being thrown from a horse during a fox hunt. He hurried to see her.

No sooner had Jane recovered from the accident than she had surgery to remove twenty-three fibroid tumors from her abdomen. "She was flat on her back for six weeks or so," Neil says. "We sort of bonded through that. I mean, I didn't run. In the past, my natural response might have been, 'Oh, okay, now that she's sick, I'm getting away.' But I was *there*.

"I kept asking myself, 'Is there anyone else I'd prefer to be with? Are there other things that I wish I was doing?' With both questions, I came up with the same answer: Jane was the woman I wanted to spend the rest of my life with. We were able to share many good times and some difficult times. We were in love and we had a strong friendship. More importantly, this person has stood by me through all sorts of things. Maybe God's trying to tell me something."

They were wed on September 16, 1990, and soon Jane, who had spent nearly twenty years believing she would never have a child, found herself discussing the option with Neil.

Both wanted a child, and medical advances had made it possible for some diabetic women to give birth. Neil "didn't expect to have a family right away." But Jane felt the ticking of her biological clock, made more urgent by the fact that the doctors had said her fibroids may return within two years.

As for the effect of pregnancy upon her diabetes, the first doctors Jane and Neil consulted advised against it. When Jane's diabetes was diagnosed in 1969, diabetic women rarely if ever had children because to do so, a diabetic needs to have normal blood sugar levels, which there was no accurate way to measure at that time. The development of monitors that yielded accurate, immediate readings of blood from a finger prick in the 1980s made it somewhat easier.

Jane faced other problems. "My kidneys were already failing. I was assured by the doctors that while they would get worse during pregnancy, they would bounce back to the poor prepregnancy levels after the baby was born.

"I was also likely to develop preeclampsia, elevation of the blood pressure, which could cause seizures, stroke and kidney failure, among other things."

Jane and Neil found a more encouraging doctor, who devised a system for Jane to monitor her blood sugar levels with a small machine. She had to maintain the levels of a nondiabetic person before it was advisable to become pregnant. This meant increasing her insulin shots and strictly controlling her diet.

"Jane and I had long conversations about the potentially negative impact bearing a biological child would have on her health. We talked to each other, we talked to doctors and, in the end, decided it was something we really wanted to try to do.

"It was a tense time because Jane had to make some serious adjustments in her regimen to minimize any complications. I knew I had to be and wanted to be as supportive as possible throughout the entire process."

Jane maintained her levels for about a year, but the regimen took a toll. For the first time, she experienced blood sugar lows that caused her to pass out. Neil learned how to give her orange juice, sugar or, if the drop was too low, a shot to bring her back.

Jane became pregnant and her kidneys worsened rapidly. Her blood sugar was stable, but she retained so much water that her petite figure swelled to nearly two hundred pounds and, in the seventh month, she developed preeclampsia and spent the last six weeks of her pregnancy lying on her left side in a hospital bed.

What worried Jane most was "that something would be wrong with the baby because of something I had done to control my diabetes. Children of diabetic women are likely to develop birth defects such as heart problems or neural tube defects, and risks associated with prematurity, such as brain bleeds and respiratory problems. I worked like hell to make sure she was all right."

Nevertheless, they were excited. "I think the part that made it worthwhile was when we had our first sonogram done: there our baby was!" Neil remembers. As for the difficult moments, "We had a really strong love and friendship that had been tested by other life changes: major surgeries and the death of my mother. I knew if we had survived those and other challenges, we could survive this one, too."

Alexandra was born via cesarean section on October 25, 1992.

When Alex was a year old, doctors told Jane to begin preparing for a double transplant: a new pancreas as well as a kidney. With a new pancreas, she would no longer be diabetic. Without it, she would simply wear out a new kidney and have to keep replacing it. She put her name on a transplant waiting list.

In 1994, Neil entered a management training program at the *Dallas Morning News*. Jane was hired as a reporter in that paper's business section, and they relocated to the Southwest.

At the end of 1994, Jane began dialysis. Three mornings a week, she went to the clinic for a four-hour treatment, then to work at the *Dallas Morning News*. Depressed by the atmosphere of hopelessness in the dialysis clinic, she urged the doctors to find an alternative. They surgically inserted a special device in her stomach and gave her a machine that allowed her to receive dialysis at night while she slept. This enabled her to resume traveling, horseback riding and an active social life.

By mid-1995, fate seemed to be working against the young family. Neil's father's health was gradually failing. Jane was still on dialysis and hoping for a transplant. Then they learned that Alex, age two and a half, was diabetic.

"It was one of the worst days of our lives," Neil says quietly.

Recognizing the need for spiritual healing, they sought solace in the church.

"I was brought up to believe that if you're a good person, bad things don't happen," Jane says. "I think maybe going to church showed me that it's not personal—bad things happen to everybody. You've just got to keep going because God's looking at you and wants you to do certain things or He wants you to learn from things. I think going to church helped me deal with this whole thing."

Shortly after Neil's father passed away in late 1995, Neil and Jane were awakened by a phone call from the University of Minnesota Hospital saying that the organs were available for a double transplant. A fourteen-year-old boy had died in a snowmobile accident and his pancreas and kidney were a good match for Jane.

Jane's first reaction was grief for the boy and his family. Then she told the doctor she was too busy to travel. "I didn't want to do it," she recalls. "I had had so many surgeries since my teens, and I wasn't ready to be cut open again."

The doctor convinced her to come. In a daze, Jane, Neil and Alex boarded a plane for Minneapolis, uncertain of what the future held.

The transplant surgery was a success. Jane began 1996 with a healthy new kidney and a pancreas that freed her from the diabetes that had ruled her life for twenty-six years. Though she had to take dozens of pills to keep her immune system from rejecting the new organs,

Alex, Jane and Neil at home

Jane was thrilled with her new lease on life. She vowed to become the best wife and mother she could possibly be.

Three months later, she awakened to the nightmare of a failed kidney (the transplanted pancreas was fine), unspeakable pain and a very uncertain future. Until Neil offered to be a donor.

A year after the transplant, Jane wrote about the experience in the *Dallas Morning News.* "This Mother's Day, I can't imagine getting perfume, jewelry or clothes. Nothing else could mean as much as that fist-sized pink filter pumping inside me that was my gift last year. Or the opportunity to truly enjoy my growing daughter and courageous husband."

Jane and Neil's love for each other is evident not only in their extraordinary bond, but in the grayer areas of everyday life. "After the surgery I thought, 'Well, I can never get mad at him about anything. He can never get on my nerves again.' "

Though they don't argue much, they occasionally disagree about their different house-keeping habits. Neil, an admitted Mr. Clean, once told Jane he couldn't marry her because she wasn't as neat as he was. While she tries to maintain his high standards, Jane laughingly says, "I have lapses, and he has to remind me."

Both dote upon Alex, whose pixie face and sparkling eyes are the perfect intersection of her parents' features. Her health is good and they take her regimen of daily shots in stride. The doctors who performed Jane's transplants are encouraged that new medical developments may someday help Alex and others with the disease.

This family's faith has been forged by adversity and strengthened with prayer. Medical advances give them new hope for the future and they treasure each moment, careful to take nothing for granted.

"I sometimes think that I'm not a good enough wife to him," Jane reveals. Neil reacts with a look of surprise. "I'd like to be better," she continues. "If I had more time to devote to him . . . like we don't talk more than five minutes before we fall asleep, or we have to schedule lunch at work so we can discuss things."

Neil shushes her with a warm gaze. "There's nothing I wouldn't do for her. No one's closer to me than she is. I want her to be a part of everything I do."

Then Alex, a small, bright symbol of her parents' love, commitment and faith, cartwheels across the floor. Jane scoops her onto her lap for a long squeeze.

Neil smiles at the women in his life. "When it gets down to it, Jane and Alex are really what define my world, no matter what I do at work or whatever else I do in life. That's what it means to have a wife and child."

FI-HANKRA

AN ENCLOSED OR SECURE COMPOUND HOUSE

A symbol of brotherhood, safety, security, completeness and solidarity. Fi-hankra is suggestive of one type of Ghanian building style that the Akan prefer. The basic concept and theory typifies protection against outside elements.

Newly wedded bliss

TOGETHER IN THE HOUSE
AND HOME

Sandra Stevens Jackson and Jesse L. Jackson, Jr.
Washington, D.C., and Chicago, Illinois

In their most heartbreaking moment, Sandra Lee Stevens Jackson and Jesse Louis Jackson, Jr., found a new dimension and purpose to their seven-year marriage and their lives. Though he lived only a few moments, the child they joined their middle names to call Lee Louis Jackson, born four months premature, strengthened the bonds of his parents' love.

Their marriage has always been good, Jesse, Jr., says, but knowing their son made it better. "Just the depth of my feelings for Sandi and the opportunity to see her, myself in someone else . . . this little person, changed the quality and quantity of our lives."

"To have met our son really focused us," Sandi says. "When he passed, it was like being shaken up. It made the importance of having a family paramount in our lives.

"You wake up and say, 'What have I been doing all this time?' "

Jesse, Jr., says losing their son caused him to consider quitting Congress. "I've said it publicly and I've said it privately: I'd leave Congress in a heartbeat if what I do for a living comes between me and Sandi. I wasn't always aware of that."

171

Their lives, split between Washington, D.C., and Chicago, are a whirlwind of nonstop activities, requests and demands. With a marriage that exemplifies teamwork, the young Illinois Democrat and his politically savvy wife are making their mark on Capitol Hill.

Some folks may assume that the son named after the celebrated father was born to shine in the political area. But the young congressman, known in Chicago as "Junior" until he won the election, says he had no such aspirations.

And Sandi hadn't exactly planned on becoming a politician's wife.

Growing up middle-class in Akron, Ohio, she wanted to be an actress/singer/dancer, then an ob/gyn. In college, she pursued journalism, then worked in television promotions and news for NBC in Toledo and the Washington Independent News Bureau in Washington, D.C.

While she was interviewing Congressman Mickey Leland for a Houston TV station, he asked her to be his press secretary. She accepted. After Leland's death in an airplane crash, she was press secretary for the Democratic Senatorial Campaign Committee and for Michael Dukakis's 1988 presidential campaign. She has also served as director of VIP relations for the Presidential Inaugural Committee and as the national outreach coordinator for the Clinton/Gore 1996 campaign.

Two years into their marriage, the couple—both law school graduates—found themselves working at the Reverend Jackson's National Rainbow Coalition. Sandi was a legal consultant. Jesse, Jr., an unordained graduate of the Chicago Theological Seminary, with unspecified plans to "do good by the Lord," served as national field director. He enjoyed and planned to stay in his job, which, in a dead-on impersonation of his dad, he describes as "keeping hope alive, never surrendering, keeping the faith."

As Jesse, Jr.'s mother, Jacqueline Jackson, had done decades before, Sandi had a vision for her husband that exceeded his own.

"I just thought, 'This guy is so talented and so intelligent, and there is a lot that he could bring to the Second Congressional District in Illinois.' Because I had worked for representatives Cleo Fields and Mickey Leland, I knew what it took to be a congressman on a day-to-day basis. I just knew that Jesse, because of his special talents, would lend himself to that office. He kept saying, 'Honey, that's *your* dream for me; that's not my dream for me.'

"I said, 'That's because you don't understand how much help a member of Congress can be to people in need.'

"After I talked to him about it for two or three weeks, he agreed to run."

According to Jesse, Jr., "Sandi helped herself to managing my campaign." She started out as his scheduler, but they quickly realized that it wasn't wise to have the candidate's wife telling prominent folks that he didn't have time to see them. She concentrated on her role as supportive spouse—and key adviser—instead.

Fueled by a desire to fight for economic security, Medicaid and Medicare and to help residents of his economically diverse, largely Black South Side district, Jesse, Jr., battled three very high-profile opponents. Though he had generous celebrity contributions, a theme song

The Reverend Jesse L. Jackson, Sr., oversees the wedding kiss.

Jesse, Jr., and Sandi during her pregnancy with Lee Louis

("Jesse Jackson, Jr., he's the one, the reverend's son, to be a congressman") and an aggressive, youth-oriented voter registration drive, it was "a tight race to the very end," Sandi says.

Flanked by Sandi and his family at his swearing-in, Jesse, Jr., informed his congressional colleagues of his goal to be known as a "freedom fighter in the character and best tradition of Martin Luther King, Jr., of Nelson Mandela and my dad, Jesse Jackson, Sr."

He's quick to credit his brainy, beautiful wife for making sure he had that opportunity. "Sandi encouraged me to be more than I wanted to be."

Perhaps it was a sign of things to come that the young couple met in Congressman Mickey Leland's office in 1987. Sandi, unimpressed, thought Jesse, Jr., was "nice." He, on the other hand, fell instantly in love. "I was totally taken by Sandi. I said, 'I can marry this girl.' She brightens up any room she walks into. She's knowledgeable, well-read, a perfect conversationalist—"

"I was a chatterbox," she says with a laugh.

"I wanted someone who was independent. I knew my spouse, whoever she might be, would have to be able to face a certain amount of scrutiny. Plus"—he smiles and gives her a flirtatious look—"she's *fine, uh uh uh*!"

Working together on a press conference, he won her over with his warm humor. Most important, he became her friend. From his home in Chicago and hers in D.C., they talked daily on the phone. "I wanted a relationship with Sandi to last. This wasn't fly-by-night where she was just gonna be my girlfriend. Both of us wanted to cultivate that and we were willing to go very, very slow."

When people on Capitol Hill learned of their friendship, Sandi says, "I had a couple of friends caution me, " 'This guy has a lot of girlfriends. You'll never be number one; he'll never be serious with you.' I was really shocked by that," Sandi continues. "Because everything people said to me about him was so *wrong*. He was the most down-to-earth, grounded, focused, well-rounded young man I had ever met. He pursued me with such vigor—it was the most romantic thing."

Their first kiss didn't come for a year and a half. Sandi was in Texas working for Michael Dukakis. Jesse, Jr., who had never sent her flowers, sent five dozen roses to work for her twenty-third birthday. Then he called and told her to wait at the office for an evening taxi delivery. Standing in the shadows, he watched her retrieve several gifts from the taxi, including a big teddy bear. When she turned and spotted Jesse, Sandi burst into tears. He kissed her, then took her to dinner.

"I love you" came six months later. Then, on his twenty-fourth birthday, while both were in law school, he slipped an engagement ring on her finger as she slept. She awakened, "saw the ring and started crying," she says. "I knew something was going on because Jesse was so nervous the day before. He had the sweats; he was not himself. I thought he was coming down with something and tried to give him some medicine. He said he was scared I would say no."

But there was no danger of that. "I couldn't imagine his not being my friend and, ultimately, my husband," Sandi admits. "Because he did everything he could, everything within his power, to build my trust in him. He bent over backwards. He put a separate phone line in his house that was just for me. Anytime that phone rang, he answered, 'Hi, sweetheart,' and that was before caller ID. I was the only person who had that number and I couldn't believe that he would go to such great lengths to assure me that I had his undivided attention."

Sandi said she never felt the weight of Jesse's family fame until it was time to meet Mrs. Jackson for the first time. "I was extremely nervous. I wanted very much to impress her." Sandi was relieved to find Mrs. Jackson warm and gracious, and "we had a great time. We're both very strong and determined women who believe very strongly in our families."

Jesse, Jr., and Sandi had known each other three years when, on June 1, 1991, a trio of ministers—the Reverend Jesse Jackson, Sr., Reverend Willie T. Barrow and Reverend Clay Evans—joined them in matrimony before about a hundred family members and friends at Jesse's Chicago home.

Sandi's younger sister, Rita Stevens Christie, made them a wedding gift of a polished gold and mahogany fertility doll from Ghana. Sandi and Jesse, Jr., now have eight such dolls, which are believed to bring good fortune and many children.

Which is what they are praying for.

"Bringing a life into this world is a most incredible gift. It's a blessing that is to be taken very seriously," Sandi muses.

As they moved through the grief of losing their first child, Sandi and Jesse, Jr., wanted to turn their pain into something positive. "One night, we were talking about what little Lee had given us by his very presence and what we could do to honor him," says Sandi. "And Jesse suggested that we create a foundation in his name to help defray the costs that parents of premature babies have to pay to keep their babies on life-support systems."

Sandi, who quit her position as senior coordinator for public diplomacy programs at the U.S. Information Agency early in her pregnancy, says she will devote a lot of time to raising money for parents such as those they met during their hospital stay.

The rest of her time is likely to be spent at her husband's side. The Jacksons are a couple who thrive on togetherness, and never seem to tire of each other's company.

"We put our relationship ahead of our careers," Jesse, Jr., says. "It's the number one priority. "I'd quit everything I do just to be with Sandi. I love every breath that she breathes. . . . We go hunting, we go fishing, we work out together, ski together. . . . I go bowling with Sandi, who cannot hold a bowling ball. I no longer need the boys; my wife does everything with me. The happiness I have here in Congress and where we live, she's responsible for that. And now she has a desk right next to mine in my office."

Colleagues say the Jacksons are affectionate, down-to-earth and frank in their admiration for each other. At a news conference where Jesse, Jr., was speaking, Sandi listened as a spectator raved about her hubby's brilliant speech. Finally, she turned to the man, adding, "And, he's cute, too!"

Sandi knows well the pitfalls of Capitol Hill. "It's a horrible drain on family life. It could have been harder on us had I not worked up here before and had an understanding of how this place works. When the Congress is in session, they're in almost six days a week. They typically start legislative business at about five in the afternoon, which means they can be here until after midnight.

"And because Jesse has a perfect voting record, he's here. It's an awesome responsibility, because so much is expected of you. Hardly a day goes by when someone doesn't come up to Jesse, Jr., or myself and thank us for something that he's done for them or something that his father and his organization have done. We're grateful that God has blessed us to be able to help so many people."

When it comes to politics, Sandi says she and Jesse, Jr., see eye-to-eye "on almost everything." But they recognize the value of disagreement.

"Sometimes we start out at opposite ends of the spectrum, but we take each other's advice and talk to a lot of people,"

Sandi and Jesse, Jr., in their dating days

says Jesse, Jr. "Sandi is part of every policy meeting in this office, so we arrive at a consensus and a decision that we can all live with."

In private, Sandi confides, Jesse, Jr., likes to talk stuff. "He can always make me laugh, even when I'm angry with him."

"But when I get to Congress, I have to be a respectable gentleman," he teases. He's serious about staying connected to his constituents. The baby-faced representative does not wear the pin that identifies him as a congressman. He wore it when he first took office, and found that folks on the Hill were cordial and respectful. Then he took it off to experience life as an anonymous Black man.

That may mean he's seen as someone to fear or pass by. Or that taxis ignore him on the street. "That's OK," he told *USA Weekend*. "In my district, I represent a lot of young African American males. Not wearing the pin reminds me of the task at hand."

Mindful of more personal priorities, the Jacksons have to "lace romance in between the work hours," Sandi says. "We try to make every minute count."

When asked to complete the sentence, "When I think of him/her, I . . ." Sandi and Jesse, Jr., spontaneously burst into *The Wiz* theme song in unison:

When I think of home, I think of a place where there's
love overflowing . . .

Then they laughed about their unrehearsed response.

"When I think of him, I really do think of home," Sandi says.

"Don't steal my answer!"

"Be quiet, honey," she jokingly scolds. "Excitement is the first thing that comes mind. He excites me in so many different ways, but the most important way for me is intellectually. I think of everlasting friendship because, no matter what, he is first and foremost my absolute best friend in all the world. He's my soulmate, my life partner. He's my lover and he's my spouse. And ultimately, the father of little Lee, who looked just like him."

The congressman turns serious.

"Sandi has taught me the meaning of honor, respect and character. Everything that I am today and everything that I will be, I owe to her, my 'Boo.' It's her capacity to grow, her capacity to understand, her capacity and willingness to build," he says.

"I have no secrets that I keep," he continues, "nothing about me that she does not know. Nothing about mistakes I've made that I have not told her about and we have endured. The greatest honor that she has given me so far, and will hopefully give me in the not-too-distant future, is family."

Becoming parents was "an awakening," says Sandi. "Everything we do now is with an eye towards how it's going to affect our children when they come. Where we live, our friends, the kind of people they will be raised around. When I carried Lee those five months, I wanted to make sure we were doing everything possible to give this child the best start. I wanted to make sure that I was being a helpmate to Jesse, and he to me, so we're presenting the best possible face of marriage to our children, so that married life wouldn't be something they would shun, but something they would embrace and look forward to."

EBAN

FENCE

A symbol of safety, security, love. A home with a fence, which symbolically separates and secures the family from the outside, is considered to be an ideal residence.

Jacci and Mel in St. Martin

TWO LIVES FEED ONE LOVE

Jacci Thompson-Dodd and Mel Dodd
St. Martin, French West Indies

Jacci Thompson-Dodd and Mel Dodd's twenty-year marriage has been a series of adventures, challenges and lessons well learned. Their knowing glances and gentle banter suggest that they are true soulmates whose destinies were meant to intertwine.

At first impression, they appear to be total opposites. She's a Gemini—multitalented, full of ideas and vision, with a knack for blending creative noncomformity and a serious head for business. He's a Virgo—down-to-earth, sizing you up while he wins you over, his razor-sharp wit couched in a soft, precise voice. Probe more deeply, though, and you'll find that they both savor the sensual pleasures of travel, sumptuous food and fine wine, and crave new adventures. Each look and touch they exchange reveals the sizzle of a couple who are not finished discovering just how delicious their love can be.

Part of their delight is a shared affinity for life off the beaten path. Growing up in prominent families, Mel Dodd and Jacci Thompson each marched to a different drummer and longed for someone who understood their beat. "We've always lived in a rather unconventional way," says Mel. "Even before we got married, we both headed in a different direction than other folks. Fortunately, we met up on the same path."

Their introduction was all but arranged between their folks, who traveled in many of the same circles. Jacci's parents, Dr. Vertis Thompson, an Oakland, California, physician, and Mary, a health educator and philanthropist; and Mel's aunt and late uncle, Russell Gideon, a Seattle pharmacist, and Lillian, a psychiatric social worker, were leaders both in their professions and in an array of Black professional and social organizations.

The Thompsons and the Gideons seemed interested in getting Jacci and Mel together. At a party in 1975, Mr. Gideon "kept showing me this picture of his nephew, Mel," Jacci recalls. "I said, 'Ooh, who is *that?*' " When Jacci's mom introduced her to Mel a year later, it took Jacci a minute to realize he was the man from the photo. "After all, my mom and I have such different taste." Jacci laughs. "I hardly expected she'd be the one to bring me my soulmate!"

Their first date was, Mel says, "more of a courtesy" to their families than anything else. Both were seeing others and had no plans to get serious. But as they chatted, they discovered that beneath their similar upbringings, both were free spirits in search of adventure, expression—and companionship.

While they appreciated their families' achievements and social standing, "We didn't pledge fraternities or sororities and I wasn't in the Cotillion," Jacci says. "Mel didn't join the Masons or The Boulé. But exposure to these things gave us a good starting point to explore other options, both separately and together."

"We talked a lot about not fitting into large social organizations, about feeling like loners." Mel laughs. "It was so comfortable from the beginning, sharing so much in common. We had the same taste in music, art and food. We read the same books and shared the same worldview. We had endless conversations about things like integrity, respect and loyalty."

"As a result, our friendship developed very quickly," Jacci adds. "There were so many things that we didn't have to explain to each other. So we started off communicating on a much deeper level, kind of 'kindred spirits.' "

Converting from Christianity to Buddhism and joining the Soka Gakkai (an international lay Buddhist organization) in 1975 was a significant turning point in Jacci's development. "Back in those days, people thought it was odd," she says. "But I didn't care. It was liberating to find a spiritual practice true to my own sensibilities."

Though Mel liked Jacci a lot as a friend, he didn't think of her as someone to marry. "In fact, I was such a loner, I just assumed I'd never get married," he says.

But Jacci intrigued him. One day while watching her immersed in her Buddhist prayers, he realized that her disciplined commitment to chanting twice a day "said a lot about her character. I told myself, 'I'd better not let this one get away so quickly.' That's when I realized she wasn't just my good friend, but might possibly be my wife."

About a year into the relationship, Jacci made a religious pilgrimage to Japan. "My sincere prayer was to have a loving, caring, monogamous relationship. I wasn't praying, 'Please give me this man.' Rather, I wanted to become the type of woman who could attract that kind of relationship. During that trip I got really clear about my dreams for the future and myself. With the knowledge in hand, Mel emerged as a man of vision and integrity. I didn't think, *'Ooh wee, I'm in love!'* I thought, 'This is the kind of person I want to be with in my life.' "

Soon after Jacci's return to the States, they really jelled as a couple. "When she got back, she was shining," says Mel. "I always thought she was beautiful and smart. But now she seemed to have a real glow about her! The love part really started clicking after that."

"Something clicked for me, too," says Jacci. "I felt more grounded and sure of myself. Deserving of a serious relationship with someone like Mel."

It wasn't long before their commitment to each other was tested. Mel got a series of job opportunities that took him first to Seattle, then to Kansas City, with the National Collegiate Athletic Association. He traveled frequently for work, which required the sweethearts to rendezvous in a variety of cities. They had checked out potential wedding rings on their travels together. But no one had popped the question. When Jacci visited Mel in Kansas City during Christmastime 1978, she took a ring he had admired in Toronto, and a new attitude.

"I was saying to myself, 'Look, I have followed this man all over the world. I have been totally devoted for three years. . . . If all of this is not demonstrating any sense of worthiness then, hey, later for this.' This was my last trip. I had the ring in hand. It was either going to be a wedding ring or a friendship ring; that was up to him."

During New Year's Eve dinner at the famed Savoy Restaurant, Jacci noticed that Mel seemed nervous. Just before dessert, he said he wanted Jacci to be his wife. "And he handed me a little box with a card that said, 'I love you and I look forward to spending my life with you. I just wish I could afford a whole carrot.'

"I opened up this beautiful velvet case and inside was an actual carrot slice carved into a little ring. It was so funny! Then he handed me another box, which had the real engagement ring. When we got back to the house, I showed him the ring I'd bought him in Toronto. He was kind of blown away that we both had marriage on our minds. So happily, I left Kansas City engaged."

On July 28, 1979, Jacci and Mel were married in a Buddhist ceremony—a first for their family and friends—in San Francisco. "The traditional altar was festooned with baskets of tropical fruit and flower offerings," Jacci says. "At first the guests felt a little strange removing their shoes and hearing the chanting," Jacci says. "But the whole thing was so warm and energized that everyone bonded, not just us!"

Mel, who was raised in Seattle's Mount Zion Baptist Church, says, "Even though I wasn't a Buddhist, our wedding was one of the most beautiful events and days of my life. When I saw Jacci and her father coming down the aisle, I swelled up with emotion."

One of the highlights was the *san san kudo* ceremony of silent vows, in which the husband and wife each drink saki three times from three different cups to symbolize their connection from the past, in the present and for the future. As Mel and Jacci stood before the altar, the leader read:

A man and wife are as close as body and shadow, flowers and fruit, or roots and leaves in every existence of life. Insects eat the trees they live in, and fish drink the water in which they swim. If grass withers, orchids grieve; if pine trees flourish, oaks rejoice. Even trees and grass are so closely related. The hiyoku is a bird with one body and two heads. Both of its mouths nourish the same body. Hiboku are fish with only one eye each, so the male and female remain together for life. A husband and wife should be like them.

—From "Letter to the Brothers" gosho.
(Gosho are sacred writings by Nichiren Daishonin to his disciples.)

In fact, Jacci's ring is engraved with the inscription, "Two lives feed one love."

Following a honeymoon in South Lake Tahoe and Santa Barbara, Mel stayed in Kansas City and Jacci in Oakland. They still got together on the road. "Because Mel was traveling so much with his job, I saw him more by us living in different cities than I would have if we lived together. I consider the whole first months of our marriage a honeymoon." Then she relocated to Kansas City.

"When we actually set up housekeeping in the same city, it was quite an adjustment," says Jacci. "We spent our courtship years on romantic weekends in exotic cities, with fancy hotels, room service, champagne and silk. Now we had our modest little home in 'mid-

Jacci and Mel at their Buddhist wedding

America' and the daily chores of married life. Added to that, we had lived independently and had our own careers established. So in some areas we were both set in our ways and that can't help but rub sometimes," Jacci admits.

After years of long-distance romance, "It took a while for us to really gain our own style as a couple. Reality doesn't have to be a letdown, though," says Jacci. "In fact, we look back on that first year of marriage with fond memories. At first, we were both brutally honest, not with the intent of being vicious. We just didn't know any better. That's when we learned to let go and be vulnerable to each other."

After a year together in Kansas City, it was clear the area lacked the lifestyle and career opportunities the Dodds desired. They headed to Seattle with no jobs, confident that they could make their way. For a while, Jacci took a job as a cook, and they lived in the basement apartment of Mel's Aunt Lillian and Uncle Russell's home. They built successful careers, Jacci in public relations for several high-profile tourism and cultural organizations, and Mel in administrative law, contract administration and the development of women and minority-owned businesses. Along the way, they bought an elegant home on Lake Washington.

They indulged their love of travel and, in 1978, made their first visit to Jamaica. Both wanted to explore a predominantly Black country with tropical weather, beautiful beaches and more natural rhythms of life. "Even before that trip we realized—separately and together—that we had an affinity for the Caribbean," Jacci says.

"Although I never met my father, my mother's husband was from Jamaica, and I always wanted to visit," says Mel. Through the years, Jacci and Mel worked hard, traveled for pleasure, and nurtured their dream of living an island life. They fell in love with St. Martin, a thirty-seven-square-mile island split between Saint Maarten, Netherlands Antilles (a department of Holland) and St. Martin, French West Indies. In 1989, they bought a home on the French side, which they used for vacations and family retreats. Even when it wasn't clear exactly when they would be able to move, they had no doubt that one day they would live there.

Like most long-married couples, Jacci and Mel had to adjust to each other's growth. Although their ability to communicate is one of their strong suits, one such change reminded them of the need to keep the lines open.

In 1987, after five years of wearing braids, Jacci decided to lock her hair. "It got to a point that wearing extensions seemed as foreign to me as processing my hair. I needed my outsides to reflect this evolving consciousness of my natural self. Wearing locks was a way to express this deepening pride and dignity I was feeling. So I did it. Problem is, I didn't discuss it with Mel first. I guess I was so into my own good feelings about myself, I never considered Mel's feelings. He wasn't too happy about it."

"It was just announced to me," Mel explains. "I think that was one of the few times in our relationship that we hadn't talked about such an important issue. It came off to me like a hasty decision that had come out of nowhere. That's what bothered me, not how she was going to wear her hair."

Jacci hadn't held back purposely. "It's not that I refused to talk about it. It's that it was kind of a spiritual unveiling that I didn't have words for," she explains.

"We were both hurt and confused by each other's reactions, and times got tense for a while. I knew I wanted to remain true to this wonderful new feeling I had inside, and share it with him in some way, too," Jacci continued. "So I prayed for a solution."

On Valentine's Day, Jacci gave Mel a favorite Buddhist book with relevant passages highlighted, along with a card and letter rededicating herself to more open communication. That gesture touched off a deep discussion that ended with Mel's support for her decision. Now, he glories in his gorgeous wife's waist-length locks.

"I've observed other couples where one person tries to find out what is sacred to their partner and then they'll challenge them on those things that are sacred, and pit themselves against those things to see how much the other person values them," Mel explains. "Jacci and I are aware of what is sacred to each of us and we respect that."

"We love each other in a way that we encourage each other to grow and explore life," Jacci adds. "And because we live this way, we've developed tremendous trust, which is one of the most valuable commodities in a marriage. Because you value that trust so much, you take extra care to behave in such a way that no one can misconstrue your intentions. Caring and respecting each other so deeply is an aphrodisiac that constantly feeds you."

That caring has helped them face more daunting challenges. One was Jacci's recurring struggle with endometriosis, a condition in which pieces of the uterine lining move into the other parts of the abdomen where they fill with blood and cause intense pain. "It's an insidious disease," Jacci says. "Aside from the physical agony, it can also keep you from feeling attractive to your spouse."

"I felt so bad for her," Mel says. "She had so many surgeries and so much pain. I felt helpless. It was a rough time for us both."

Mel was Jacci's silver lining. "Through it all, he was so wonderful. He always found ways to make me feel loved and desirable. Sometimes he would help me laugh—or cry—when I needed to. Mostly, he made it clear that he supported me and would be there, no matter what. In times like these, you come to treasure the fact that your mate knows you, sees you at your very worst, and still loves you and wants to be with you. *That* reality, *that* caring, is really validating."

Surprisingly, Jacci and Mel learned that as a result of Jacci's many surgeries, they would be able to become parents. "Because of my health history, I had assumed we'd be childless," says Jacci. "To have a choice was a little unsettling at first."

After talking about it long and hard, "we finally decided to try and have a child," Mel says. "After thirteen years of marriage, we didn't want to lose ourselves on the baby-making trail, but we figured it was worth a try."

On June 4, 1992, their daughter Nailah ("one who succeeds") Cayenne Dodd was born. Now that they are parents, they agree, they can't imagine life any other way.

One of the reasons they wanted to move to St. Martin, Mel says, "is that we wanted our daughter to have an image of us enjoying a life that wasn't so stressful. Back in the States, we were so bound up by our professional obligations that our family life was beginning to suffer." In 1998, thanks to careful planning and judicious saving, Jacci and Mel were able to walk away from their demanding jobs to live on St. Martin with the goal of putting peace of mind and family unity first. "It was important for Nailah to see that if you have the determination, you can achieve your dreams," Mel says. "And as a Black child, it became important for Nailah to be exposed to many different cultures to better prepare her to become a citizen of the world."

"Raising our child with an understanding that people come in all 'wrappers' without the judgment of which one is 'better' is a gift we wanted desperately to give her," Jacci says. "This is a very diverse environment, a true mélange of cultures, where you're as likely to hear French, Dutch, Spanish, and varied Creole and patois dialects as you are English."

As they prepared to finalize the sale of their Seattle home for the move to St. Martin, the Dodd family faced a shocking challenge. During a routine physical exam, Mel was diagnosed as having H Pylori with evidence of a cancer called Malt Lymphoma.

"That day in the doctor's office was a nightmare," Jacci recalls. "I remember the two 'C' words—cancer and chemotherapy. That was the saddest, most tearful walk to the car we ever had. We cried a lot together over the next two days. Mel was afraid of missing out on Nailah growing up. Every time he looked at her, he started to cry. It was agonizing."

"Initially, we had very little information regarding Malt Lymphoma," Mel says. "We weren't sure how to respond or react. It seems again the Universe provided us with the resources. I not only had a specialist in Seattle, but through Jacci's father, consulted with an oncologist in the Bay Area who is a recognized expert in treating Malt Lymphoma."

The offer on their house fell through and they rushed to cancel their moving plans and re-establish the basics of life in Seattle. Mel was put on a course of medications and the doctors allowed them a monthlong visit to St. Martin to mellow out. They returned to Seattle for more testing and treatments. Finally, they got the word that Mel's tests were negative and the cancer was gone. Soon thereafter, another, better, offer on their house came through, and they were able to move.

The experience, Mel says, helped him "gain some wisdom in learning how to better prioritize things in life. What became most important was living in the present and in that, valuing to an even greater degree my wife, daughter and interpersonal relationships. It was strange for me because I tend to be such a detailed—some say picky—person. During that time, most of those things that I had previously been concerned with became trifling and trivial. I realized they were a waste of my energy. I really enjoyed seeing my daughter off to school each morning and taking walks with my wife. Or just sitting in the same room with her and saying nothing."

Jacci says that she "felt a range of emotions I had never experienced before—from intense depression to soaring ecstacy. I found I was much stronger than I ever realized. I really became appreciative for every day and every breath. Life became much sweeter. More precious."

The Dodds faced more adversity when Hurricane George hit St. Martin in 1998. "There were 110-mile-per-hour winds churning around the island for over twelve hours," Jacci says. "Through it all, we were safe and our house was left untouched. But uniting as a family in the midst of this thing that we had no control over brought us even closer."

Mel and Jacci view their laid-back life in tropical paradise as the natural evolution of following their instincts. "We listen to our spirits. We've wound up in the places we wanted to be in life mainly because we've had faith in the Universe. In the cosmic plan, not just our own."

Jacci says she feels that their spirituality "had a lot to do with us coming together and staying together. Whenever we have determined to work at something, even though our approaches aren't exactly the same, we always seem to get there together."

Ironically, Jacci says, "there was a part of me that was really attracted to the perception of Mel being 'settled' and 'stable' " in the beginning of their courtship. "At the time, because he was in the 'right' job and all that, it seemed like the strength of his character was manifested by the fact that he was living a responsible life. But we've grown beyond that. Now I realize that his real strength shows in his willingness to walk away from all that. Some may think that quitting our jobs, selling our belongings and leaving the States is crazy. But we're happier."

Tropical life, while pleasant in many ways, requires some serious adjustments, Jacci says. "Life here is very slow. The glacial pace of getting business done would frustrate most Americans; it frustrates us too, sometimes. For now, it's the price we're willing to pay to get our spirits fortified."

Every moment of their time together, Jacci says, "reminds me of what an extraordinary man I'm married to. He's a wonderful friend, adventurer, husband and father. It's an honor to share my life with him," she says.

Mel responds. "Left to my own devices, I don't know where I would have ended up." "Thanks to powers greater than me, Jacci came into my life. She's definitely the right mate for me in this lifetime."

Their intertwined fingers, deep caramel and rich chocolate, hint that when kindred spirits come together, the results are simply divine.

AYA

THE FERN

This popular Adinkra symbol represents endurance, independence, defiance against difficulties, hardiness, perseverance and resourcefulness. A fern is a rugged and hardy plant that flourishes, survives, and grows in unusual and sometimes harsh terrain. The Akan liken people who flourish and survive to the properties of the fern plant. Such a person does not sway from the direction of his or her goals.

Rick and Michele in the Adams Morgan neighborhood of Washington, D.C.

WALKING THE WALK

Michele and Richard "Rick" Tingling-Clemmons
Washington, D.C.

Many folks talk about trying to make the world a better place. Michele and Richard Tingling-Clemmons turn talk into action every day. Their ongoing quest for justice fuels their work, their family life and their marriage.

At their 1983 wedding, Michele Tingling and Rick Clemmons pledged to work together for equality for all people in all walks of life and promised to instill the same convictions in their children. They danced to live African drumbeats, exchanged spontaneous vows and jumped the broom in memory of slaves who were forbidden to legally marry. Then they joined their surnames in a gesture of loving solidarity.

Just as they have kept their promises to build an everlasting love, they have made a difference in the lives of others. These world-class political organizers have worked—for pay and for free—in Cuba, China, Japan, Nicaragua, Switzerland, Sweden and forty-five of America's United States. They have brought together diverse groups of people seeking solutions to such problems as hunger, homelessness, environmental justice, war, racism, lack of education, unsafe workplaces, nuclear bombs and reactors and unrest in developing countries.

They work to instill their three youngest children with a global sense of right and wrong, an understanding of justice that works in their home, school and neighborhood as well as outside the United States. "We live in an era where we have the technological capability to provide the basic necessities and comforts for everyone on this planet," Michele says. "Therefore, we have a responsibility to work on behalf of people in communities everywhere, particularly children. That's why, in our household, community organizing is a family affair."

They opt to live in the 'hood in northeast Washington, D.C., because they want to stay close to the people they work with, and keep in touch with the issues that concern them most.

The couple arrived at their shared convictions from very different places. Rick hails from a large, Norfolk, Virginia, family that enjoyed a middle-class lifestyle until Rick's entrepreneurial father died. The sudden change in lifestyle persuaded Rick that he wanted to be a millionaire by age thirty-five, which he expected to achieve through hard work and honesty. Midway through the Vietnam War, he joined the Air Force with an eye on a free college education. When he was sent to Japan, he asked to go to 'Nam because combat pay was higher.

While taking business classes at the University of Maryland Extension College in Tokyo, Rick read fliers handed out by anti-war demonstrators. He began to question his goals, beliefs and place in the military. He asked other students and professors about his country and the war it was involved in. Their reply—that capitalism was a bigger problem in America than racism, that class rather than color caused inequality—blew Rick's mind. He changed from an aspiring millionaire to "a soldier in service to the people."

In the military, Rick became part of the anti-nuclear and anti-war movements and the Black Panther Party. He spoke and demonstrated openly against the war, but left the Air Force with an honorable discharge.

He did social work and founded a drug rehabilitation program in Norfolk. Now, in addition to teaching high school social studies at Young Technocrats, an African-centered math and science public charter school for pre-K through twelfth grade, he does community and political organizing, researches educational- and urban-affairs issues and consults with a variety of community-based organizations. He has a bachelor's degree in urban studies and a master's in adult education from the University of the District of Columbia, and is a Ph.D. candidate in sociology at Howard University.

Michele is a New Yorker, the only daughter of an attorney (later judge) father and school-teacher mother who reared their three children to question authority, contest history and recognize injustice. At fifteen, she was graduated from the Bronx High School of Science and received a scholarship to Wellesley College. There she helped organize her fellow Black students to confront college officials with their demands and helped found a Black student choir and the Black Studies department.

After graduating, Michele knew that she wanted to change the world, to right society's wrongs. The sight of people suffering made her sick and strengthened her determination to make sure they had what they needed to live decent lives.

At Richard Jr.'s wedding. Seated (l to r): Rick's first wife, Mitsuko; Rick and Michele's son, Langston; Richard Jr.'s wife, Ann; Rick and Mitsuko's son, bridegroom Richard Jr., Rick.
1st row standing, (l to r): Christopher Diggs; Rick's sister, Gloria Fox; Mimi's godmother, Kyung Hee Barnes; niece Delta Clemmons; nephew Frank Clemmons, Jr., Rick and Betsy's youngest daughter, Christine; Michele; Rick's adopted daughter, Debbie; Mitsuko's cousin, Kimiko; Rick and Mitsuko's daughter, Mim; Rick and Michele's son, Toussaint.
Back row (l to r): Rick and Betsy's daughter, Marlen; Jim (Rick's brother-in-law), Betsy's partner, Dr. Jim Diggs; Rick's second wife, Betsy Smith; Rick and Betsy's son, Mao; great-nephew Frank II (on his shoulders); Frank, Jr.'s wife, Sharon Clemmons; Kimiko's sons, Leon Sherrell and Loren Sherrell; and Debbie's husband, Roy Alexander

She worked at some New York high schools and various social service agencies. Then, at twenty-five, she moved to Washington to become the first salaried employee for the struggling Urban Environment Conference and an early advocate for environmental justice, which involves identifying and correcting unsafe living conditions in poor and minority communities. Since 1985 she has been a senior field organizer for the Food Research and Action Center, a nonprofit agency. She is admired for her drive, diligence, positive attitude and ability to confront folks in power.

Michele's and Rick's work has taken them around the globe. In 1984, Rick went to Nicaragua to protest U.S. government funding of the Contras as part of a Veteran's Tour. In 1993, he spoke at the World Conference Against Atomic and Hydrogen Bombs in Japan, and organized discussions at the Conference Against Xenophobia in Geneva, Switzerland.

Michele visited China in 1995 to attend the Fourth World Conference on Women, where she was part of a diverse delegation of African American women, the largest group at the event.

Together, Rick and Michele attended the National Convention of the League of Revolutionaries for a New America in Chicago, a multiethnic group working to spread the idea that technology should help, rather than displace, human labor.

Both Michele and Rick find joy in the battle for social change and satisfaction knowing that they agree on what's most important in life. They surround themselves with people who share their belief that the best hope for their children's future lies in working for a new, more equitable world. And when they get tired or discouraged, they are there for each other.

This righteous love began with a wrong number in 1982. On a winter day in January, Rick, who is dyslexic, was calling a woman friend to confirm a lunch date. He transposed the numbers and rang Michele. She listened—amused—as he chatted on. When she advised him of the mix-up, he said he'd call back to start the conversation over. Fat chance, Michele thought, in the days before most phones had "redial" buttons. "He doesn't even know who he's talking to."

He called back ninety seconds later.

Michele was alternately encouraged and daunted by their first conversation. "He said wonderful things like, 'I think that the families are really the building block of society,' so I'm thinking, 'That's really great!' Then he says, 'I've been married twice before,' and I'm like, 'Oh God, he comes with baggage!'"

"He says, 'My children are the most important people in the world to me . . .' and I'm thinking, 'Great!' and he said, 'And I have six of them,' and I'm thinking, 'Oh, *big-time* baggage.'

"Then he says, 'I'm a revolutionary,' and I'm thinking, 'That's fantastic. I can't believe I found somebody on the *telephone* who's a revolutionary!' And he said, 'I used to have affiliations with kind of crazy political organizations and I was one of the founding members of the Revolutionary Communist Party.' And I said, 'And he's *crazy,* too.' But I was never bored. One of the things I always feared wasn't so much how do you find somebody, decide on the correct mate, but how do you find somebody who will never bore you?"

Rick's romantic résumé was anything but boring. It included marriage to his Japanese first wife, Mitsuko, with whom he has two children, Richard "Bo" Clemmons, thirty-two, and Mitsuko "Mimi" China, twenty-seven, and a longtime common-law union to his White second wife, Betsy Smith, with whom he has three birth children, Mao Tse-Tung, twenty-four; Marlen, twenty-one; and Christine, twenty. Rick considers Debbie, a forty-one-year-old white woman whom he adopted when she was a troubled teen in need of a legal guardian, part of his family as well.

In 1979, while Rick's relationship with his second wife was ending, he found her with another man in his home and felt that the man was a threat to his family. In an uncharacteristic flash of anger, Rick grabbed a gun and wounded the two of them. Both fully recovered and now live together. Rick served over a year and a half in prison for shooting them.

Rick revealed the shooting early on to Michele, earning points from her for honesty. He told her that if he ever again reached a point in a relationship where he felt that the only way to resolve an issue was through force or violence, he would simply leave.

Michele, who felt some trepidation, says she thought that might take more self-control than he was capable of. "But I was still willing to take risks," she says. "I found that there were a lot of other dimensions to him, so I was willing to keep an open, wait-and-see attitude."

A devoted part-time father who saw his children regularly, Rick was on a mission to find a mate. "I promised myself that my next wife would be African American, with compatible politics." Michele became a prime prospect as they got to know each other by phone. "A lot of our discussions were like a marriage interview," he says. "I really wanted to know her, and she told me honestly what she felt."

Michele, meanwhile, had concluded "that the chances of me finding a man and settling

Easter Sunday, 1998, Mt. Morris Ascension Presbyterian Church, Harlem, N.Y.
(from left) Michele's baby brother, Steven Adair Tingling; cousin Makeda Tingling with
daughter, Makea; Michele; Toussaint; Langston; Michele's mother, Eunice; and Rick.

down in a monogamous relationship were probably limited, because all the men that I was interested in were already involved in relationships or had lot of baggage."

When Rick first called, she was dating "a very eclectic group of guys. I wanted a man who was political, who thought that family was important but that building a family was also part of your political work. I wanted somebody like me who has a passion to change what I see as a really unjust society. I wanted a big man and Rick sounded *huge* on the phone. And I wanted a man who was dark-skinned, because I've always wanted to be really dark."

They spent a couple of weeks getting to know each other by phone, picking some fights, Rick admits, to see if they were compatible.

When they met in person, both were immediately captivated. "He wasn't a big man, but he had this smile. . . . There used to be this toothpaste commercial where this couple would start running toward each other and when they smiled, the gleam from their smiles blinded them and they put their hands up and ran past each other. That's how I felt when he started grinning, and every time I looked at him I would catch him smiling again and it was infectious. . . ."

Rick, already infatuated with Michele's mind and spirit, appreciated her statuesque curves and affinity for going barefoot.

For the next several weeks, they got to know each other over lunch dates. "I loved having these political discussions, feeling like I wasn't under any pressure to establish a relationship, being able to be open and to actually express my ideas," Michele says. They worked together on several political projects and demonstrations, organizing the first Jobs with Peace activities in 1983 and the Washington, D.C., section of the April Action for Jobs, Peace and Justice national march in 1985.

In the process, Michele realized that a relationship with Rick would be anything but casual. "I either had to go for it or keep him at a distance. In the meantime, he never pressured me. We weren't intimate yet, but we had gotten very close."

He was dating two other women at the time, but once Rick saw how Michele hit it off with his kids, he knew that she was the one.

They began living together and Rick later proposed that they have kids. Was he talking about marriage? Michele asked. No, he said. Her own reply that she wasn't having kids outside of marriage surprised her because she never considered herself conservative.

"He said, 'Okay, I'll marry you,' I said, 'I don't think so. That's not how you ask me.'" It took Rick several months—and many formal proposals—before Michele accepted.

Some people asked Michele whether she really wanted to marry a man with six kids. "It was sort of a package deal. One thing that attracted me to Rick was his devotion to his children. It would have been hypocritical of me to say, 'I love the fact that you love children, I just don't want you to love any except the ones that we have together.' Plus they are such great kids."

Michele and Rick were wed on June 12, 1983, at the Crispus Attucks Museum and Park of the Arts, a community museum filled with African art. A gay White male Unitarian minister friend officiated. "We weren't Christians, but our families are, so we wanted to have a minister and we wanted him to talk about Jesus Christ as a revolutionary because that was one of the things that inspired us," Michele says. Shunning gold or diamonds from apartheid-era South Africa, they exchanged specially designed rings of Tibetan silver.

Rick says, "I married Michele because she had all of the things that I wanted in a woman." One of those things was an instinct for mothering. "There was never a moment after those first visits that I didn't think that Michele would be a great mother to my early kids and that she would be a wonderful mother" to any children that they conceived.

Rick and Michele went on to have three children of their own: Toussaint L'Ouverture, fifteen (named in honor of the Haitian revolutionary); Nzingha Michele, thirteen (named after an Angolan warrior-diplomat queen, and her mom) and Langston Mandela, eleven (named for the poet and the first South African president).

"We see the raising of our family as our most serious political work 'cause that's where our legacy is," Rick says. His view that "there is only one race, the human race," is exemplified in his multicolored offspring. Proud of their diversity, they are bound by their father's blood, a fierce devotion to each other and a high level of social consciousness.

"I just love my stepchildren," Michele says with a smile. "Everybody has their differences, but they're very open, honest, loving kids. They were brought up to accept the fact that their family included everyone, not just those who lived in their immediate household."

Toussaint, Nzingha and Langston share their parents' strong sense of social justice. "They take it personally when they see somebody on the street who's homeless. They want to do something about that, because they think there's something that they *can* do," says Michele.

While rich in love, this activist couple has a modest income and is well aware of how poverty can damage couples and families. "One of the main things that breaks up relationships is economic conditions," Michele observes. "When do you have the most fights? When the money is funny; when one of you is worried in a different way than the other one about how you're gonna make your bills that month and what are the repercussions of not making it."

"I think that people lose sight of what they mean to each other because part of the key in marriages or relationships is the economy," Rick agrees. "It spills over into other things. I think people don't make it because they don't know that."

One thing Michele and Rick know is how to debate their way through their own disagreements. "There is a lot of passion in our relationship because neither of us gives in easily, both of us have tempers," Michele says. "Our ideas express a lot about us, but we need to remember that just because we express an idea that the other one finds offensive doesn't mean that we're not the same person who loves and cares for that person."

Michele says marriage has helped her to become more capable in many areas, from sharing financial decisions to learning the rhythms of parenting. "I have grown in this relationship. I've grown in my effectiveness as a community activist. Even our struggles in the relationship make me strong, make me better."

Rick listens attentively as Michele speaks, and she returns the favor. Their eyes caress each other's face as ideas and words swirl between them. "Michele never ceases to amaze me, even today," says Rick. "My respect and love for her grows because of the work we're doing."

The Tingling-Clemmonses continually challenge themselves and everyone around them to "walk the walk" toward a new and better world. They replace rhetoric with activism, remain committed to beliefs that many others gave up on long ago, and strive to live directly from the heart.

"Our love is still in the struggle and in our appreciation for the different things that we see in each other and it's still about difference," Rick says. "Our love is a moving and active love; it's fun and intriguing."

Michele is quick to second that emotion. "I'd say our love is exciting, it's ever-growing; it's anything but static. It's productive, it's challenging and I wouldn't trade it," she concludes.

As they join their hearts in romance, clasp their hands in struggle, embrace nine children representing three continents and leave their footprints on paths of progress all over the globe, Michele and Rick Tingling-Clemmons are enjoying a truly revolutionary love.

NKYINKYIN

TWISTINGS

A symbol of toughness, adaptability, selfless devotion to service and an ability to withstand hardships and difficulties. The capacity to adapt to circumstances is much admired by the Akan people. Change is often the vehicle by which we come out ahead.

Adeyemi Bandele and Iyanla Vanzant at their wedding

SOUL CONNECTION

Iyanla Vanzant and Adeyemi Bandele
Silver Spring, Maryland

Do you want me to be in your head or in your bed?" she asked when he suggested that they move from friendship to romance. "You have to make a choice."

It wasn't the first time that Iyanla Vanzant and Adeyemi Bandele had been at this crossroads. Twelve years earlier, in 1984, the longtime friends and colleagues were working on a project in Brooklyn, New York. Adeyemi had just ended his marriage and Iyanla was coming out of a relationship.

She was a spiritual counselor to him and others, advising him about ending a long-term relationship. "We were sitting in a car at the ocean, and he asked if he could kiss me," Iyanla remembers.

"I was clear that I couldn't be his counselor *and* his lover. 'You have to make a choice,' I told him. He said, 'Okay, I'll take the bed.' And because I had been attracted to him for such a long time, I said, 'This is a gift from God.' "

Iyanla had wanted Adeyemi since she first set eyes on him at a summer job program in Brooklyn twenty years before. "I was fourteen, he was seventeen," she recalls. "He was tall and thin; I was short and fat. He was very quiet and gentle. I was very aggressive and boisterous." A computer error messed up her paycheck; Adeyemi was the counselor assigned to help straighten out the problem. He was patient and comforting and she fell hard for him.

"Of course, I couldn't have him. He was seeing a girlfriend of mine and totally oblivious to the fact that I was madly in love with him."

Time passed. Adeyemi became a successful grassroots organizer and teacher at an independent school. Iyanla danced in an African dance troupe and worked on community projects. Living and working in the same neighborhood, their paths often crossed. He broke up with Iyanla's girlfriend and married someone else.

And Iyanla longed for him all the while. As she wrote in *In the Meantime: Finding Yourself and the Love You Want*:

> Other people had me convinced that what I felt was not love. They said it was infatuation. Because they were older and, I thought, wiser than me, I believed them. I thought it best to ignore what I felt . . . I concluded that we would never, could never be together . . . that I was not good enough to be loved by him or anyone . . .

At sixteen, she fell for a guy who got her pregnant, then left her. When he came back three years later, she was convinced she had found love, and she married him. She says her husband cheated, beat her, broke her ribs and jaw and walked out on the day they were supposed to move into a better apartment, leaving Iyanla and her three children homeless and desperate. She unpacked the box marked "bathroom" and took every pill inside.

She awoke in a hospital, surprised to be alive. And determined to stay that way. As she writes in her books, she feared being alone and believed that finding the right man was the answer. She had no trouble attracting men—some gorgeous, some loving—all, ultimately, just out of reach, as her father had been while she was growing up. Every relationship taught her something and each disappointment helped her grow. Iyanla was extraordinary in that she was able to transform these terrible experiences into insights that she shared with others.

Meanwhile, Adeyemi was "involved in an extended family—what some people call a 'polygamous' relationship," he says, with two women, one with whom he had five children.

In the mid-1980s, he recognized Iyanla at Medgar Evers College, where she was student body president. Working together on various projects, they got to know each other better.

Adeyemi says he was touched by her compassion and commitment to helping others, and impressed with her intellect and abilities.

"She was someone I could really talk to on a genuine level," Adeyemi recalls. "I came to know her skills and creativity. She's just a waymaker in so many respects. Whatever the challenges, her capacity to overcome them and find some creative ways to make them happen is what really enamored me. And, of course, she's very attractive and an absolutely incredible conversationalist."

In her quest for spiritual growth and healing, Iyanla had been told that she was destined to be a minister. Years before, she had grown tired of Holiness church ministers telling her that everything was a sin. She was attracted to the faith of the ancient Yoruba people of Nigeria, West Africa, which was practiced in the homes of priests rather than in church, and, as Iyanla says, helped her understand God in a way that made her feel good and didn't frighten her.

Iyanla's studies led her to become a Yoruba priestess, which involved a weeklong initiation process and a year of studying the sacred scriptures of the Yoruba people, along with herbs, the planets, numbers and ways in which to make the mind, body and spirit whole.

Both of Adeyemi's committed relationships ended around 1984. Despondent, he visited Iyanla. She, too, had just ended a relationship. Adeyemi shared his woes and she counseled him until the moment at the ocean's shore when he asked for a kiss.

They ended up in a "very intense relationship," Adeyemi says, "one that was marked by a lot of sharing, by our dedication and caring for each other. It was that kind of rhythm and connectedness that kept us together."

They got an apartment. "He had weekend custody of seven kids from seven or eight years old to fourteen or fifteen," Iyanla says. Their children, some of whom were the same ages, "bonded and blended—it was a family."

After a year, Iyanla moved into a nearby apartment with her ailing mother, for whom she was caring. She juggled the relationship with Adeyemi, her responsibilities to both her mother and children and law school.

Adeyemi felt guilty about his first family and, three-and-a-half years into the relationship with Iyanla, he started seeing his first wife again. "My transition . . . was not done as it should have been done. I didn't bring closure to one relationship before going into another, and it was very painful for both of us."

Iyanla says she "fell apart . . . I was just raw, devastated."

They saw each other on occasional weekends for nearly two years. It was difficult for her to accept being "the other woman." Then he broke that off. "And that's when the real crisis began," she says.

Devastated, Iyanla spent the next ten years trying to figure out why the man she had spent most of her life loving didn't want to be with her. She moved her family to Philadelphia, where she practiced criminal defense law and furthered her personal growth.

"Without spiritual education, I would have been a basket case. This was a man who was emotionally unavailable to me, just like my father. A man who loved me and didn't know how to express it . . . a good person who had stuff he had to work through, just like my father.

"My journey became to make peace with my father." This was a long and complex process for Iyanla, who, in her books, describes her father as a troubled man who was emotionally and physically abusive and withheld his affection from Iyanla and her brother, Ray.

During this process, she realized she had to let Adeyemi go. "It took me about three years to say, 'I can love this man and feel good about him whether or not I'm with him. We may never be together, but that doesn't kill the love.'

"Once I did that, we started talking again. I was no longer holding him responsible for my pain. I was more concerned about healing myself than I was about mending the relationship."

Adeyemi divorced his first wife and moved with four of his sons to Atlanta. By this time, Iyanla was a published author living in Silver Spring, Maryland. "I was hearing about her work, still very proud of her. I always spoke very highly of her."

When Adeyemi became committed to someone else, Iyanla, focusing on her own growth, "was very happy for him. I was with myself and totally at peace with it, and I wasn't looking for somebody to make me happy."

She continued to attract men who were physically present but emotionally distant, breaking up with them when she recognized the pattern.

In 1996, Adeyemi's relationship hit a crisis, and he turned to Iyanla for advice. "If you want to know the end, look at the beginning," she says. "We were right back in the same place as in 1984: I had ended my relationship; he was ending a relationship, and I was supporting him with that."

She told him that he needed solitude in order to heal. He decided to spend a year by himself. "I had reached a stage where I really was looking for a very serious commitment and a monogamous relationship, I think, because of the spiritual quest," he explains. "I just wanted some order and stability in my life. I didn't want to cause anybody anymore pain because of my own lack of discipline in my behavior."

Iyanla supported his decision. "We were talking every day but my head was still into 'there's not anything going on here.' " Then she went to Atlanta on business and he met her plane.

"There was a look, a touch, a moment in the airport," she recalls, "and I still ignored it because he had made a commitment to be by himself for a year and I wanted to be real clear that I was functioning as a support arm."

Near the end of the year, in a phone conversation, they found themselves back at the crossroads: friends or lovers?

The question was the same, but the people asking it had grown. "I was really adamant that he needed to heal," Iyanla says. "So I said to him, 'I know that I'm not going to have another relationship with a man until I'm married. I'm tired of that; I'm too old; I'm not doing that anymore. So if you're not ready to make that kind of commitment, just forget it.' "

He was ready, he assured her, and suddenly they were discussing the possibilities. And the requirements.

Because Iyanla is a Yoruba priestess, Adeyemi had to ask her elders if they could marry.

With both parents deceased, Iyanla's elders were her godfather, Ogun Kunle, of Atlanta, and the woman Iyanla calls her spiritual mother and mentor, Dr. Barbara Lewis King, founder and minister of Hillside Chapel and Truth Center in Atlanta, a nondenominational Unity church with a congregation of about five thousand.

Adeyemi went first to Iyanla's godfather, who then called Iyanla to Atlanta so the three of them could talk. "I thought my godfather was going to say to me, 'You've got to leave this alone,' and I didn't want to hear that," she admits. "I went to Atlanta and sat with them and the next thing I knew, Adeyemi was on his knees, asking me to marry him.

"My godfather said he would be honored to give his daughter to Adeyemi. He said 'Y'all have a soul connection; you've had it for a very long time and anybody who knows you and sees you knows that this is something much deeper than just the physical thing. If you're coming together at this time in your life, after you've both matured and grown, it's really something that needs to happen.' "

Dr. Barbara King cautioned Adeyemi, "God has something very special for Iyanla to do and she can't be stopped in her work. So if you're thinking that you're going to get a wife that's going to be cooking and cleaning and taking care of you, you can forget that. I want to know what is your vision for yourself because she already has her work and her vision cut out."

After an intense discussion, and some prayer, Dr. King gave the couple her blessing.

"My elders were keeping me clear and focused," Iyanla says. "I knew that it was different because it never looked like this before. I was finally healed, because I was willing, if either one of them didn't support the marriage, to let him go. That was a major, major piece for me because my pattern had been to do *anything* to keep the relationship.

"Yemi knew that I was real clear. He was willing, too. We understood that we could be friends and love each other and we didn't *have to* be married. We were *choosing* to be married."

They traveled to Nigeria for Adeyemi to become prepared to wed a woman of Iyanla's religious stature. It would have been awkward for her, a Yoruba priestess, to marry a man who had not been initiated into the religion. "We would not have been equally yoked spiritually," Iyanla explains.

"The roles were really reversed," Iyanla notes. "In my case, it was the man who had to be prepared for the woman. He was ready, very open and willing to do whatever it took to solidify this marriage."

After a series of Yoruba rituals, Adeyemi was initiated as a high priest in the Yoruba tradition. Although he was not on the same level as Iyanla, this gave him access to the highest level of spiritual rites.

They had a Nigerian wedding ceremony involving eighteen other priests who did a form of divination to learn the couple's destiny, including the challenges they would face and what they would have to do to overcome them.

Despite the bond of their Nigerian wedding, one of those challenges almost shook the foundation of their commitment. While planning their U.S. wedding, Iyanla, best-selling author and spiritual guide to thousands of people, came face-to-face with her own deeply rooted fear of unconditional love.

In *In the Meantime,* she wrote:

I had experienced a total transformation in my consciousness and my life that I openly attributed to the activity of God's unconditional love in my life. I was the author of four books, had conducted workshops, seminars, and given lectures across the country on a wide variety of matters and topics, all of which were based on the concept of unconditional love. I thought that I was unconditional love in heels! Then into my life walked a man who declared unconditional love for me. I immediately went into shock, fear, and a mode of self-destruct.

She found fault with Adeyemi, looked for evidence of his wrongdoing, reasoned that something must be wrong with him if he wanted her. He just kept telling the truth, keeping his word, honoring their commitment and showering her with romance.

She knew that he was a good man and a devoted father, committed to spiritual growth. She appreciated his loving kindness, generosity and ability to express his emotions. Still, she became even more critical, questioning his motives and character. When she asked for space, he gave it. When she pointed out her flaws, he replied, "That's what I love about you most!"

After doing everything in her power to drive him away and debating whether to call off the wedding, she asked herself why she was attacking him. Hadn't she always loved Adeyemi and wanted to be with him? Wasn't he the man she had visualized, affirmed and prayed for?

Taking the advice she gives others, she stepped out on faith, planning a large, lavish, outdoor ceremony—while writing two books and moving her business into another building.

Adeyemi, an accomplished event organizer, found it challenging to let Iyanla take the lead in coordinating their big day. "The first lesson was being able to release and let go," he says. "Then I developed the capacity to say, 'Yes, Dear.'"

They were married on May 10, 1997—Iyanla's late father's birthday—on an estate in Columbia, Maryland. The weather was cold and gray until the bride and groom reached the altar, resplendent in purple and gold African attire. The sun came out and they recited the vows they had written, under the watchful eyes of a Yoruba priestess, an Akan priestess and Dr. Barbara Lewis King, with Baba Ishangi, who Iyanla describes as "a master teacher and cultural custodian," officiating.

The wedding party included their ten children, along with longtime friends and mentors. There were supporters and skeptics in the crowd of two hundred.

"We had drummers and dancers, and we moved through the ceremony with Yoruba chants," Iyanla says. "We sang to Oshun, the deity of love, harmony, peace and joy. The audience had to dance. In accordance with Yoruba tradition, they had to agree to certain things, like not to talk about us. They had to agree that, if they saw difficulties or challenges in the marriage, that they would correct either one of us or themselves.

"They had to answer questions about us: 'Do you know him to be a man of honor? Do you think that this marriage is an asset to the community?' The men had to answer questions for him; the women for me. And the community had to affirm its support of this marriage. Because you don't marry an individual, you marry the family and a portion of the community."

Soon after, the couple had some unexpected revelations about their state of matrimony.

"I thought I was choosing to be married to my best friend," Iyanla says, "to someone that I knew I loved at a soul level and because I thought it was the next step in my growth and development, about being able to love at a different, deeper level. I had already demonstrated that I could do it on my own. I didn't *need* to be married for any reason.

"After we got married, I discovered that I was doing it to prove to people that this was gonna work. And that I was doing it to heal at an even deeper level."

The first year, she admits, "has been challenging. We've been forced to grow out of our comfort zones and to really examine ourselves."

Prior to the wedding, they lived in different states and agreed that, since Iyanla's business and staff are in Maryland, Adeyemi would relocate from Atlanta. They discussed his role in her business, Inner Visions Spiritual Life Maintenance Network, and how they would complement each other.

Based on past experience, they assumed that working together would be a breeze. They didn't realize how much they—and the energy between them—had changed.

"I was no longer needy, codependent or silent, and my first commitment was to God," she says. "So whereas Adeyemi's ideas had always been to me like dewdrops from Heaven, now I would say, 'Wait a minute. What principle is that? Let me pray on it.' It became very frustrating.

"I made the decisions; I make the money; I run this ministry," she continues. "I had been the man *and* the woman for so long . . . that to actually allow a male being into my life was very challenging. Although he may have had a good idea about what to do and how to do it, instead of there being a man and a woman in the room, there were two men. Our egos clashed. He's a grassroots political organizer and everything is for the good of the people. I'm a minister, a priest and an executive director that takes direction first from God. Our process was very different."

There were other differences as well. Adeyemi, having come out of a succession of relationships, was "real conscious about communication. If I'm out late, I call to say I'm on the way in—things one generally takes for granted when one has a partner."

Iyanla had been on her own for so long that she was not accustomed to answering to or discussing her plans with anyone. She is learning, though, that "when you have a life partner, you have to have that discussion and take the other person's feelings into consideration, whatever you're doing. For me it's a challenge because I haven't had to do that.

"The other big thing for us is that he knows that God comes first in my life. And that, as a wife, you have to examine your [commitment to God coming first] and you have to keep that in balance, but it's also a boundary that you have to maintain."

Then there is the issue of privacy. "We have husband-wife business that I don't talk about," she says. "But he knows that if he does something, if we have a challenge or argument or discrepancy and I learn something that can help one person, it's gonna show up in a book."

One of the biggest challenges for Adeyemi has been coping with role-reversal culture shock. In Atlanta, he had lived with his sons, and by 1996, they had finished high school and returned to New York. "Finally, I had a house to myself—free—my *own* space," he says. He could immerse himself in his favorite music, and in his work. As a consultant, planner and organizer, he enriched Atlanta's cultural scene and helped to establish the Atlanta African Crossroads Festival and a Tribute to Our Ancestors program.

"I was active; I had my resources, my network and was very grounded in that community," he says. "So when I moved to Maryland, that was a major adjustment. I was now married to somebody very famous. I was working in Inner Visions, the institution that Iyanla had established, and we were staying in her home. I no longer had my own base."

Moreover, he was "completely in awe of Iyanla—not the author, the famous person—but the person *I* knew, with no makeup on in the morning, and I just absolutely love her!

"My focus was on the relationship and her. Her focus was on her writing, her work and her mission. We were like AM and FM. The first time around, the focus was on *my* work and commitments." This time, he says, he gave his all to supporting Iyanla's work. "And that wasn't what Iyanla was looking for," he says.

"It became real stressful. I didn't have my own sense of who I am. I made the mistake of not producing and listening to music, which is the vehicle for my spirit. I was not engaged in doing the things that kept me grounded. All of that stuff converged and created some serious blockage."

Fortunately, the couple has life coaches, ministers, counselors and their elders to help them work through the conflicts.

"We're blessed; this is a community marriage with people invested in it, and we've got a lot of love and support around us," Iyanla says. "When things get rough, our coach asks us how this can bring us closer together."

They moved out of her place into one of their own and Adeyemi is getting centered with music and other soul-satisfying activities. "Prayer and being in a spiritual environment has been a saving grace, because it's real clear that the Creator is an active part of this relationship and not a Band-Aid," he observes.

"We are both clear that our marriage is a service to God and we are just the tools being used, so it is important that we hold God in the center of the marriage," Iyanla says. "The coming together of a masculine and a feminine expression of God and everything we do has to be for and in service to God, and that bumps the relationship up to a whole 'nother level."

They agree that, unless there is dishonor (such as infidelity), violence or abuse, leaving is not an option. "We know that God has brought us together not in body, but in spirit, to do something very important—our own individual healing. When the healing becomes painful, we don't have the options of saying 'I don't want to deal with this!' and leaving," Iyanla says.

Although they love each other deeply, they both realize that a successful marriage requires more. "I think in relationships sometimes the question is not 'Do you love this person?' but 'Do you *respect* this person?' " Iyanla observes. "One thing Yemi and I have always had is a respect for one another. When you respect somebody, you can tell the truth knowing that, even if they don't like it or it makes them angry, they need to know it. We may not want to hurt them because we love them, but with respect you can tell them the truth no matter what, because the respect and admiration are still going to be there."

Adeyemi has learned that "the bottom line is commitment and willingness. Because you can be madly in love with somebody but you can't live together day in and day out.

"The other important piece is the community," he continues. "You've got to have some people you share with. Not the girlfriends you call to complain to, but people you respect and go to for assistance, people you open up and surrender your stuff to."

While the bond that has taken them from a summer youth program in Brooklyn to a marriage anchored in spirituality and blessed by villages on two continents is "joyful and exciting, it's also frightening," Iyanla admits. "Because when I think that another human being knows me and loves me anyhow, it just takes my breath away."

MUSUYIDEE OR KRAPA

"THING" FOR SACRIFICE

A symbol of spiritual balance, good fortune, good luck, sanctity, spiritual strength and the uprightness of spirit. It is, in essence, a cross, a sign to remove evil, a sign of spiritual balance or spiritual cleansing. Musuyidee is also the name of a ceremony used to bring luck.

Recommended Reading

We enjoyed reading the following books in the process of researching *A Love Supreme,* and encourage you to savor them.

Burnett, Jr., Zaron W. *The Carthaginian Honor Society.* Atlanta, GA: A publication of Just Us Theater Press, a Division of Just Us Theater Company, Inc., 1991.

Cleage, Pearl. *Mad at Miles: A Blackwoman's Guide to Truth.* The Cleage Group, Inc., 1991.

———. *Deals with the Devil and Other Reasons to Riot.* The Cleage Group, Inc., 1993.

———. *What Looks Like Crazy on an Ordinary Day.* New York: Avon Books, 1997.

Cole, Dr. Johnnetta B. *All American Women: Lines That Divide, Ties That Bind.* New York: The Free Press, 1986.

———. *Anthropology for the Eighties: Introductory Readings.* New York: The Free Press, 1982.

———. *Anthropology for the Nineties: Introductory Readings.* New York: The Free Press, 1988.

———. *Conversations: Straight Talk with America's Sister President.* New York: Doubleday, 1993.

———. *Dream the Boldest Dreams: And Other Lessons of Life: A Book of Aphorisms.* Marietta, GA: Longstreet Press, 1997.

Davis, Ossie, and Ruby Dee. *With Ossie & Ruby: In This Life Together.* New York: Morrow, 1998.

Dee, Ruby. *My One Good Nerve.* New York: John Wiley & Sons, Inc., 1987.

Elders, Dr. Joycelyn, and David Chanoff. *Joycelyn Elders M.D.: From Sharecropper's Daughter to Surgeon General of the United States of America.* New York: Morrow, 1996.

Evans, Mari. *A Dark and Splendid Mass.* New York: Harlem River Press, 1992.

Graves, Earl G. *How to Succeed in Business Without Being White: Straight Talk on Making it in America.* New York: HarperCollins Publishers, 1997.

Powell, Colin, with Joseph E. Persico. *My American Journey.* New York: Random House, 1995.

Vanzant, Iyanla. *Acts of Faith: Daily Meditations for People of Color.* New York: Simon & Schuster, 1993.

———. *The Value in the Valley: A Black Woman's Guide Through Life's Dilemmas.* New York: Simon & Schuster, 1995.

———. *The Spirit of a Man: A Vision of Transformation for Black Men and the Women Who Love Them.* New York: Harper Collins 1997.

———. *Faith in the Valley: Lessons for Women on the Journey to Peace.* New York: Simon & Schuster, 1998.

———. *In the Meantime: Finding Yourself and the Love You Want.* New York: Simon & Schuster, 1998.

———. *One Day My Soul Just Opened Up.* New York: Simon & Schuster, 1998.

———. *Yesterday I Cried: Celebrating the Lessons of Living and Loving.* New York: Simon & Schuster, 1999.

———. *In Good Company: A Woman's Journal for Spiritual Reflection, 2000.* Cleveland, OH: Pilgrim Press, 1999.

Willis, Bruce, W. *The Adinkra Dictionary: A Visual Primer on the Language of ADINKRA.* The Pyramid Complex, 1998.

About the Authors

TaRessa and Calvin Stovall exchanged vows and jumped the broom on September 2, 1990. Their love story began when they met in 1989 at the National Association of Black Journalists convention in New York City. "I immediately jumped on the love train," Calvin says, "but it took her a few stops before she hopped on board."

In the midst of a whirlwind, six-month long-distance romance, they became engaged. A year after meeting, they were wed at their home in Atlanta. Weeks later, they were on their way to becoming parents.

Describing themselves as "a classic case of opposites attract," TaRessa and Calvin find challenges and humor in their marriage and family life. Calvin says he married TaRessa because "she's crazy and cute." TaRessa says she married Calvin because "he made me laugh on our first date, and made it safe for me to open my heart." They are involved in a loving competition to see who can have the last word.

As communications professionals, the Stovalls were frustrated at the lack of honest, positive images of African American couples and families in mainstream media and culture. *A Love Supreme: Real-Life Stories of Black Love* is their effort at filling that gap.

Calvin works as managing editor of the *Courier-Post* newspaper in Cherry Hill, New Jersey. He began his career as a news reporter at the *San Jose*, (California), *Mercury News,* and worked his way up the news ladder as assistant city editor, then metro editor, at the *News-Sentinel* in Fort Wayne, Indiana; assistant city editor, day city editor and business editor at the *Detroit News*, and assistant to the managing editor at the *Atlanta Journal and Constitution*; to senior managing editor at Gannett News Service in Arlington, Virginia. He served as a corporate news executive in Gannett's Newspaper Division in Arlington for five years before joining the *Courier-Post*. His roots are in the rural, south-central Arkansas town of Okolona, "where everyone joined parents in shaping the lives of the young," he says. Calvin earned a B.A. in political science at San Jose State University.

TaRessa, a native of Seattle, has been a writer since age seven. Her poetry has won awards and appeared in national magazines. Her plays have been produced throughout the Pacific Northwest and in Chicago and considered for Off-Broadway. TaRessa is co-author of *Catching Good Health: An Introduction to Homeopathic Medicine*, and the author of *The Buffalo Soldiers*, a young adults' book. After working as director of public relations for Spelman College, speechwriter for U.S. Health and Human Services Secretary Louis W. Sullivan, media director for the Children's Defense Fund Black Community Crusade for Children and executive director of the National Association of Minority Media Executives, TaRessa is concentrating on writing and selected communications consulting for clients such as the Freddie Mac Foundation. She earned a B.A. in media and communications writing, production and promotion from the Evergreen State College in Olympia, Washington.

The Stovalls live in Mt. Laurel, New Jersey, with their children, Calvin II and Mariah, who are busy trying to run their little corner of the world.